Twenty Observations on a
World in Turmoil

Twenty Observations on a World in Turmoil

Ulrich Beck

Translated by
Ciaran Cronin

polity

First published in German as *Nachrichten aus der Weltinnenpolitik*
© Suhrkamp Verlag Berlin 2010.

This English edition © Polity Press, 2012.

Polity Press
65 Bridge Street
Cambridge CB2 1UR, UK

Polity Press
350 Main Street
Malden, MA 02148, USA

ISBN-13: 978-0-7456-5396-9 (hardback)
ISBN-13: 978-0-7456-5397-6 (paperback)

A catalogue record for this book is available from the British Library.

Typeset in 11 on 13 pt Sabon
by Toppan Best-set Premedia Limited
Printed and bound in Great Britain by the MPG Books Group

The publisher has used its best endeavours to ensure that the URLs for external websites referred to in this book are correct and active at the time of going to press. However, the publisher has no responsibility for the websites and can make no guarantee that a site will remain live or that the content is or will remain appropriate.

Every effort has been made to trace all copyright holders, but if any have been inadvertently overlooked the publisher will be pleased to include any necessary credits in any subsequent reprint or edition.

For further information on Polity, visit our website: www.politybooks.com

Contents

Preface

For many years it has been my business to sound out the present for potential futures (something one should do, however, only with a certain twinkle in the eye). Today the question is: which opportunities, which futures are implicit in the events convulsing the world – the nuclear worst-case scenario in Fukushima, the global financial crisis, the chaos in the euro zone, the uprisings of the Arab spring, as well as the protest movements in Athens, Barcelona, New York, Moscow, etc.? This much seems clear: nobody thought they were possible. They are exploding our horizon of expectation (including the conceptual framework of the social sciences!). They are striking at the heart of modernity. At the same time they are opening up new spaces of action, including space for alliances across all borders. All of them are by nature transnational and therefore cannot be understood and explained within the frame of reference of the national outlook. And, most of all, there are uprisings of 'multiple global generations' and revolutionary middle classes, even in the United States and Russia. The *citoyen* is making a comeback across the globe!

Two diametrically opposed futures are looming. One is a Hegel scenario in which the threats engendered by global risk capitalism represent a historical opportunity for the 'cunning of reason'. This is the cosmopolitan imperative: cooperate or fail, succeed together or fail alone.

At the same time, however, the everyday experience that the world is becoming uncontrollable also triggers a Carl Schmitt scenario, a strategic power game which, as the planetary state of exception is becoming normalized, dismantles basic rights and democracy and opens the doors for a neonationalist politics. Remarkably, these mutually contradictory potential futures seem to be interconnected in a variety of ways; this used to be called 'dialectics'.

One way or another, we have to find new ways to orient ourselves in a world that is in a state of turmoil. Of course, political leaders need to address local issues and to react to people's specific demands; but without a cosmopolitan outlook, such a reaction is likely to be inadequate. My *Twenty Observations on a World in Turmoil* is a demonstration of cosmopolitan politics in practice. It is more than a mirror: it is a magnifying glass that brings into focus the processes which are transforming our world and highlights the formidable challenges we face today.

Weltinnenpolitik, 'global domestic politics', the concept I am introducing and developing, is much more than a political theory, a philosophical utopia (or dystopia), a governance programme or a state of mind: it is the reality of our times. I turn the argument that 'global domestic politics' is an unrealistic ideology on its head, arguing that at the beginning of the twenty-first century it is the proponents of the national who are the idealists. They view reality through the obsolete lenses of the nation state and thus cannot see the profound global changes which are transforming our reality. Global domestic politics is therefore a perspective, a political reality and a normative idea. And it is *the* critical theory of our times since it challenges the most profound truths which we hold dear: the truths of the nation.*

Nationalism is particularly toxic not only because of the overt justification it gives to national protectionism and global inequalities. It is dangerous on account of its cognitive status: nationalism defines and ossifies our political and social scientific frameworks and our most basic categories of thought and knowledge. Nationalism as an ideology thus limits not only what we can imagine and wish for, but, more importantly, what we know and how we conceive of reality. The most basic categories are indeed captive to the national order: family, gender, religion, class, democracy, politics, etc. – all are nationally defined. Our legal and administrative systems define them and these definitions are amplified by the social sciences. The demystification of our sciences requires us to part with nationalism and to see the world as it is, as already cosmopolitan. And indeed, climate change, financial crises, cities, migration, families, Europe, risk societies – if we open our eyes we can see that they all are already cosmopolitan. Especially world cities are examples of this reality: they are part of the world – being nodal points for the dissemination of people, goods, technologies, capital, risks and images – but are still part of their nations. They exemplify the logic of 'both/and' – of both globalism and localism, of

---

* Carl Friedrich von Weizsäcker used the concept 'Weltinnenpolitik' in a philosophical sense in a 1963 lecture in which he draws on Immanuel Kant. I lend this word a new sociological meaning. The question one needs to ask is 'What *is* global domestic politics?' rather than 'What should global domestic politics be?' The second turn I propose is a cognitive one: the national outlook misjudges reality (on this see the following and chs. 18 and 19).

the transnational that cohabits with the national – which is in fact the logic of global domestic politics (rather than 'either/or').

Critics argue that this story lacks the 'agents' which propel it. They ask: how has this global domestic politics come into being? Was it an unavoidable unfolding of an idea? Was it a side-effect of global capitalism? Who were the agents who advanced the reality of cosmopolitanism and the processes that I propose be uncovered? And isn't the puzzling blindness of various people to this reality not, in fact, a blindness at all, but an antagonism in wilful opposition to this *involuntary* global domestic politics?

Modernity is threatening to fail specifically on account of its successes – that is my thesis. Precisely the staged threat of failure – not first the catastrophe but already the anticipation of the catastrophe – is undermining the key institutions of the nation state and making the latter receptive in a new way to cross-border political initiatives. The social and psychological volatility entailed by cultural relativism, on the one hand, and the recognition of global risk, on the other, are giving rise to enormous discontent, which in turn inspires various political and social movements for resistance and reform. Those movements address – to put it bluntly – the moral aspect of the events now unfolding. The protesters, who are 'Occupying Wall Street' in different countries, are calling for a return to the principles of equality, social justice and solidarity. People are questioning why the crisis for which they are not to blame should be solved at their expense.

This might be the birth of a new '*Weltbild*', a new world view – namely, global domestic politics – because such protests and projects are typically justified in the name of 'humanity' and 'the planet'. The universality of such claims, moreover, is not conjured up out of thin air or a merely utopian aspiration. Instead it presents itself in the form of globally available cultural models of protest and resentment ('We are the ninety-nine per cent', 'occupying Wall Street'), which, when enacted by activists and social movements, inspire new circles of human agency and responsibility to change, save or otherwise repair the world in the name of 'another modernity'.

Global domestic politics includes the caveat that our orientation to the world is becoming continually more critically reflexive. At the same time – and this is crucial – it is becoming more universalistic, interventionistic, and prescriptive: the contradictions between the hegemonic universalism of the Western world picture ('the American way of life') and a new global domestic politics from below characterize open local-global conflicts over the 'good world' – and, of course, over who has the power to define it.

And there are other essential questions: will people in Europe live in a Post-Europe? What will a post-European Europe look like? Will there be new and old wars? Or will Europe be able to play a positive role if its current economic policies and its failure to cooperate condemn it to stagnation and long-term crises?

Too much is coming to an end, too little is beginning. This slim volume collects *Twenty Observations on a World in Turmoil*, published in leading European newspapers between 2009 and 2011. It represents a kind of monthly journal, miniature depictions of the future, on the question: where is the old merely being restored and where is the new being given a chance?

Munich, January 2012
Ulrich Beck

1

Mushrooms and Other Flowers of Capitalism

July 2009

For many Japanese, matsutake, wild gourmet mushrooms, are the most Japanese thing that the Japanese cuisine has to offer. These mushrooms acquire their unique flavour precisely where the environmental crisis has left its traces, in barren forests on parched ground. During the 1970s, as the anthropologist Anna Tsing reports, two things came together in Japan: increasing wealth and increasing environmental destruction. Thus, the 'wild' gourmet mushrooms had to be 'produced' and their production 'outsourced' – to the forests of China, South Korea, Sweden, Turkey, Mexico, Canada and the United States. Who harvests the mushrooms? Refugees, migrants, 'outsourced' citizens of the world and 'self-entrepreneurs' living at the edge or precipice of society, for whom living and working in ruined forests is not too much to ask. Thus the outsourcing of risks and the outsourcing of people come together in the symbol of the matsutake mushrooms, the most expensive mushrooms in the world and an original Japanese delicacy with which the Japanese enjoy their success and celebrate it for all to see. The macrocosm of globalized outsourcing capitalism is reflected in the microcosm of the mushrooms.

Thus, the 'whether' is no longer the issue. Outsourcing as a feature of global domestic politics – offloading risks and responsibility onto the weak who do the dirty work for the rich for a pittance – has become a key global source of profit in which the domination of the rich, the exploitation of the poor and the destruction of nature are entering into new combinations and becoming radicalized across all borders. The 'national vision', national borders and laws, transform deliberate outsourcing into 'latent side effects' in the no-man's-land of organized irresponsibility.

This capitalism of disposal and supply chains (Anna Tsing) permeates all domains. The major corporations, which at one time were famous and celebrated for their comprehensive production machinery, have mutated into masters of outsourcing. Governments are imitating them by outsourcing everything – from social services, through war, even to torture – to subcontractors. Scientists arrange to have research projects which are regarded as ethically suspect or are forbidden in the EU conducted in 'low ethics countries'. Moreover, the 'emancipation compromise' on which the unstable balance between double income marriages and parenthood is based in the West, falls under the headings of 'outsourcing' or 'insourcing'. The labour which many women no longer want to do and which most men, in spite of lip service paid to open-mindedness, still do not want to perform – namely, the incessant, monotonous, dirty and yet joyful work involved in family and parenthood – is being delegated to immigrant women: 'substitute mothers'.

This is one point of global domestic politics: the outside suggested by the concept of '*out*sourcing' no longer exists. A particularly drastic illustration of this is provided by the so-called 'environmental' problems. Many people still believe that these 'latent side effects' of their industrial or political decisions can be 'outsourced' across national borders to 'others', 'foreigners', who do not have any public voice and cannot defend themselves. However, this *factual* global domestic politics raises questions of *normative* global domestic politics: how can the 'outsourcing' of transnational harms be exposed and placed on the global domestic political agenda? How can the boundaries of moral and political equality be redrawn? How can the 'outsourced' citizens of the world be included in decisions which affect their vital interests?

Are we living in a neo-neoliberal capitalist system to which there are no alternatives?

One can literally hear it, the big sigh of relief on the markets. With the recent rise in the value of their stocks, the investors are already celebrating the end of the crisis. On the credit markets, too, there are muffled cries of joy – the message is that confidence has returned. Perhaps the clearest indicator is that those highly risky investments which started the whole slide are again in demand – in spite of a shrinking economy. How are banks which are still threatened by collapse able to make these megadeals? Quite simply by making the crisis itself into a business. Speculation has turned from junk assets to government bonds, in other words, to the money that the state must raise in order to rescue capitalism from itself. There are still gnawing doubts, for example that the Great Depression also only really set in in 1931 when people thought it was already over. When it comes to the present, it seemed for a brief historical moment as though the boundless, neoliberal capitalism would become reflexive and open to learning when faced with its self-endangerment.

Are the calls for regulation merely empty words? Has the window of opportunity for civilizing market fundamentalism already closed again? Could it even be that we are experiencing the shortest recession since the

Second World War, now that the players can no longer contain their jubilation? Before everything finally turns to the good, we should again recall what was actually involved and is still involved.

The twentieth century was marked by two antagonistic and mutually exclusive systems: capitalism and socialism. We lived through two experiments on a planetary scale. One of them tried to impose the model of a centralized planned state economy, the other the capitalist economy free from any controls. The collapse of the Berlin Wall in 1989 marked the failure of socialism. Now 'pure' capitalism is collapsing before our very eyes. There are good reasons for assuming that, although we are not witnessing the end of capitalism, we may be witnessing the end of that kind of neoliberal fundamentalist capitalism which held the world and its governments in thrall in the years since Margaret Thatcher and Ronald Reagan. State socialism went bankrupt also because the alternative of unregulated market capitalism existed. As a consequence, one elite could be replaced by another. The pure doctrine of market capitalism is now likewise bankrupt, but without a viable alternative – either in economics or in politics. Everywhere the neoliberal poachers were appointed gamekeepers. However, this raises the question: is it even possible for pure capitalism to go bankrupt if the old elites continue to govern disguised as state socialist turncoats? Are we living in a global system of neoliberal state capitalism that is simultaneously bankrupt and not bankrupt but to which there is no alternative?

The politics of climate change: squaring the circle

If it is the case that each of us must save the world from the impending climate catastrophe every day, then the US government under George W. Bush was actually good for something: one could blame Bush for everything that failed to occur or went wrong. Now many environmental activists hope that Barack Obama will bring about the environmental turn. In fact, the House of Representatives in Washington recently enacted a law to place limits on carbon dioxide emissions. What is envisaged may represent a giant step by comparison with the denial of climate change propagated by the Bush administration around the world. But the guidelines have actually turned out to be so moderate that they will probably have little effect. However, the Indians and Chinese, whose support has to be won for a worldwide agreement on climate change, are arming themselves with arguments that are not so easy to refute. By now, China has probably become the greatest global CO_2 transgressor; factored over the per capita income of its population, however, emissions in China are still far below levels in the West. How, the Indians and Chinese ask, can Americans and Europeans claim the right to consume energy on a scale that they want to deny to the poorer countries?

The proposal of the West boils down to the rich countries providing financial aid to the poorest states to enable them to reduce emissions by importing new, clean technologies from the West: this amounts to capitalist environmental altruism. China has made an interesting alternative proposal which is putting pressure on the Western governments: all developed countries should make one per cent of their gross national product available to enable poorer countries to combat global warming. What consequences would such an agreement have? The United States has a budget deficit of twelve per cent. The Chinese are holding US government bonds to the tune of at least $800 billion. It is they who are 'rescuing' – that is, buying up – the large companies in Europe and the United States. Imagine the following scenario: Obama would have to explain to his fellow Americans that he is issuing a large cheque to the Chinese, among others, so that they can combat climate change with clean technologies, while at the same time he must hope that the Chinese will generously buy American government bonds so that the American budget deficit can be financed!

The following squaring of the circle is in the offing: the more all sides proclaim their good will to solve the problem of climate change, and thus the weaker official objections become across the world, the more involved and contradictory the search for viable answers becomes. There is no one left to blame for the failure of climate policy. But for this very reason climate policy is at the mercy of the internal calamities of a radically unequal world. The debate on climate policy is dominated by what must and should be done – or by a green, all-party technocracy of market gullibility. If only good intentions – and their taboos – were enough!

Strange bed fellows

The hardliners in Iran are at each other's throats. This could have advantages from the perspective of the sociology of power – that is, from the civil society perspective of the Iranian demonstrators and their sympathizers. When restrictions are placed on public liberties, it is the tendencies towards fragmentation within the more or less monolithic block of the governing clergy which – as the example of Gorbachev demonstrates – could bring the whole power structure tumbling down. Iran's spiritual leader, Ayatollah Khamenei, has called upon President Ahmadinejad to dismiss the recently appointed first vice president. This was reported by the acting Speaker of Parliament, a confidant of Khamenei's. Prior to this, leading representatives of the hardliners among the clergy and in the media were harshly criticized. This has opened up a further, perhaps decisive, line of conflict in the confrontations that began with the presidential election of 12 July 2009.

Yet how is this turmoil perceived in Iran and how does it appear from the global domestic political perspective of the European Left? The freedom fighters in Iran do not respect the human rights guidelines which are indispensable in the view of the European Left. They wear green headbands to evoke Khomeini's religious revolution and to protect themselves from the brute force of the regime. And aren't they pro-American? Consumerist? Internet-conformists? Transnationally net-worked? Perhaps even drug addicts? Thus 'rent boys of financial capital' (as a Western Marxist put it) who are ultimately getting what's coming to them?

Liberation movements, human rights and Islam – these are not good bedfellows, as both the Left and the Right know from their own European experience. Therefore, it is better to keep calm so as not to jeopardize the good negotiation relations with the emerging nuclear power and the Ayatollah regime. New, disconcerting, coalitions among the various orthodoxies are emerging within global domestic politics: strange partners are climbing into bed with each other across all boundaries.

2

All Aboard the Nuclear Power Superjet – Just Don't Ask about the Landing Strip

August 2009

Climate change and the oil crisis are being used to project atomic energy as a green panacea. In fact atomic energy is a reckless gamble.

Are we witnessing the beginning of a real-life satire, at once amusing and terrifying? Its theme is the over-shadowing of the nuclear power risk by catastrophic climate change and the oil crisis. The US President and the British Prime Minister have reiterated their support for the construction of new nuclear power plants. The British government has announced the fast-tracking of eight new reactors and called for 'a renaissance of nuclear power' in a 'post-oil economy'. It is as if a world that wants to save the climate must learn to appreciate the beauty of atomic energy – or 'green energy', as Germany's ruling Christian Democratic Union party has rechristened it. Given this new turn in the politics of language, we should remind ourselves of the following.

Recently the US Congress established an expert commission to develop a language or symbolism capable of warning against the threats posed by American nuclear waste dumps 10,000 years from now. The problem to be solved was: how must concepts and symbols be designed in order to convey a message to future generations millennia from now? The commission included physicists, anthropologists, linguists, neuroscientists, psychologists, molecular biologists, classical scholars, artists, and so on.

The experts looked for models among the oldest symbols of humanity. They studied the construction of Stonehenge and the pyramids and examined the historical reception of Homer and the Bible. But these reached back at most a couple of thousand years, not 10,000. The anthropologists recommended the symbol of the skull and crossbones. However, a historian reminded the commission that the skull and crossbones symbolized resurrection for the alchemists, and a psychologist conducted an experiment with three-year-olds: if the symbol was affixed to a bottle they anxiously shouted 'poison!', but if it was placed on a wall they enthusiastically yelled 'pirates!'

Even our language fails, therefore, when faced with the challenge of alerting future generations to the dangers we have introduced into the world through the use of nuclear power. Seen in this light, the actors who are supposed to be the guarantors of security and rationality – the state, science and industry – are engaged in a highly ambivalent game. They are no longer trustees but suspects, no longer managers of risks but also sources of risks. For they are urging the population to climb into an aircraft for which a landing strip has not yet been built.

The 'existential concern' being awakened across the world by global risks has led to a contest to suppress large-scale risks in political discussion. The incalculable dangers to which climate change is giving rise are supposed to be 'combated' with the incalculable dangers associated with nuclear power plants. Many decisions over large-scale risks are a matter of choosing not between safe and risky alternatives, but between different risky alternatives, and often between alternatives whose risks are too qualitatively different to be easily compared. Existing forms of scientific and public discourse are no match for such considerations. Here governments adopt the strategy of deliberate simplification. They present each specific decision as one between safe and risky alternatives, while playing down the uncertainties of atomic energy and focusing attention on the oil crisis and climate change.

The striking fact is that the lines of conflict within world risk society are cultural ones. The more global risks escape the usual methods of scientific calculation and turn out to be a domain of relative non-knowing, the more important becomes the cultural perception of specific global risks – that is, the belief in their reality or unreality. In the case of nuclear power, we are witnessing a clash of risk cultures. Thus the Chernobyl experience is perceived differently in Germany and France, Britain, Spain, or Ukraine and Russia. For many Europeans the threats posed by climate change now loom much larger than nuclear power or terrorism.

Now that climate change is regarded as man-made and its catastrophic impacts are viewed as inevitable, the cards are being reshuffled in society and politics. But it is completely mistaken to represent climate change as an unavoidable path to human destruction. For climate change opens up unexpected opportunities to rewrite the rules and priorities of politics. Although the rise in the price of oil benefits the climate, it comes with the threat of mass decline. The explosion in energy costs is gnawing away at standards of living and is giving rise to a risk of poverty at the heart of society. As a consequence, the priority which was still accorded energy security twenty-five years after Chernobyl is being undermined by the question of how long consumers can maintain their standards of living in the face of the steady increase in energy prices.

Yet to disregard the 'residual risk' of atomic energy is to misunderstand the cultural and political dynamic of the 'residual risk society'. The most tenacious, convincing and effective critics of atomic energy are not the greens – the most influential opponent of the nuclear industry is the nuclear industry itself.

Even if politicians were to be successful in their semantic reinvention of nuclear power as green electricity, and even if the opposing social movements were to dissipate their energy through fragmentation, this is all nullified by the real opposing force of the threat. It is constant, permanent and remains present even when exhausted demonstrators have long since given up. The probability of improbable accidents increases with the number of 'green' nuclear plants; each 'occurrence' awakens memories of all the others, throughout the world.

For risk is not synonymous with catastrophe. Risk means the anticipation of catastrophe, not just in a specific place but everywhere. It doesn't even have to come to a mini-Chernobyl in Europe. The global public need only to get wind of negligence and 'human error' somewhere in the world and suddenly the governments advocating 'green' nuclear power will find themselves accused of gambling recklessly and against their better judgement with the security interests of the population.

Given that radioactivity is invisible and odourless, what will become of 'responsible citizens' who cannot perceive these threats produced by civilization, and hence are robbed of their sovereign judgement? Consider the following thought experiment. What would happen if radioactivity caused itchiness? Realists, also known as cynics, will answer: people would invent something, for example an ointment, to 'suppress' the itching – no doubt a profitable business with a good future. Of course, convincing explanations would immediately be offered explaining that the itching was unimportant, that it could be traced back to factors other than radioactivity. Presumably such attempts to explain things away would have a poor chance of survival if everyone ran around with irritating skin rashes, and fashion shoots and business meetings were accompanied by incessant scratching. Then the social and political ways of dealing with modern large-scale hazards would be confronted with a completely different situation because the issue under discussion and negotiation would be culturally visible.

3

This Appalling Injustice!

September 2009

San Francisco, early August 2009. I'm taking a stroll through the streets around the Hilton Hotel where this year's American sociology conference is being held. Sociologists, like casualty surgeons, are a pretty callous lot. Crises are their stock-in-trade. The people catch my attention. Over there one of them is lying on the side of the street, a policeman does a quick check for signs of life and continues on his way. Many of them have to struggle against the contortions of their own bodies just to keep moving. We're sitting in a Vietnamese restaurant having lunch, delicious food, window seats. Suddenly, out of nowhere, a large, gaunt figure clad in tattered rags fills the whole window like an ominous bird, delighting in the fright that he (or she, it's hard to tell) is causing. The waiter routinely chases him or her away like an annoying, neighbourhood dog that everyone mistreats. Across the way someone is lurching across the busy street, oblivious of the beeping horns and screeching brakes of the traffic streaming past. The glazed-over eyes in the bodies coming towards me, some of them grotesquely obese, others wasted away almost to nothing – roughly one in ten of those I encountered – are still etched in my memory.

This appalling social injustice! Even in the global economic crisis, the wealthy pay at worst in the value of their stocks, whereas the most vulnerable social groups, who have nothing to do with the crisis, are 'paying' for it in the hard currency of their so-called existence. Here we are no longer dealing with 'the poor' – the concept is too weak. To speak in terms of 'class' would be a cynical euphemism. 'Wasted lives' is what Zygmunt Bauman has called them in a profoundly disturbing analogy to the mounds of waste being permanently churned out by the ever-sleeker and more efficient engine of capitalism. Bauman speaks of the invisible sub-cities in which these 'wasted humans' are vegetating away. In light of this, does the fact that they are conspicuous everywhere on San Francisco's main thoroughfares already represent progress?

Abject poverty rubbing shoulders with wealth is certainly nothing new. But today, under conditions of global domestic politics, it represents an appalling injustice, now that social equality has become a worldwide expectation and the growing inequalities can neither be justified as willed by God nor be hidden behind the walls of the nation state. But it is also a moral problem, for me, for my generation. Our reproach to our parents was: how could you have known nothing about the atrocities of the Nazis?! And today? Thousands of world citizens are drowning off the coast of the EU, millions of children are starving to death every day. But we look away. That is at once trivial and deeply outrageous.

The sociologist in me says: that is far from the end of it; the forgotten regions and countries must fear still greater neglect and devastation. And all of this is known – and nobody is shocked. It merely shows the relativity of human outrage.

Yet this is precisely what has become false. In global domestic politics the legitimation which made this relativity of outrage possible is crumbling. The poor are made poor not only by their poverty but also by the flows of information which make their situation comparable. They are becoming 'our' poor and they become poor because they know about our affluence. The more norms of equality gain worldwide acceptance and the more emphatically and successfully the West promotes human rights, the more global inequality is losing its foundation of legitimacy in institutionalized disregard – albeit in the form of a one-sided asymmetry: the poor no longer accept the incomparability based on nation state borders; they compare themselves with the West – and want to get in!

The wealthy countries protect themselves by clinging to the illusion that nation states cannot be compared with each other. They focus their compassion and their outrage on their 'own' national poverty. Thus the illusion of incomparability is also contributing to increasing numbers of people in the rich countries feeling poor or threatened by poverty.

Global domestic politics means that the poverty of the poor is becoming a political scandal not only through growing poverty but also through the universalization of equality. Now everyone can see that their poverty is the precondition of our wealth, that the inhumanity of their condition presupposes and places in question our high-flown claims to humanity. However, this recognition holds more for the poor. For the rich, it only suffices to give them a bad conscience – and even that rarely enough.

In the evening, back in my hotel room on the thirty-fifth floor with a stunning view across the rooftops of San Francisco to the Golden Gate Bridge, I'm watching a TV report about a medical charity event. It's hard to imagine a message more diametrically opposed to the public hysteria stirred up against US President Obama's healthcare reform. A black woman, who has waited all night with her twelve-year-old son to wrangle an every-morning ticket for free dental treatment, is being interviewed. She has dental problems and has difficulty remembering the last time she visited a dentist. For she faces a stark alternative: 'It's a simple choice – either I pay the rent or I pay the health insurance.' Her son also has dental problems. Hundreds of people are waiting here resignedly for their big chance to finally have the most urgent medical repair work done on their bodies free of charge. The people lining up here patiently with their children have often travelled hundreds of miles. They are not the poorest of the poor; they are more likely to belong to the lower middle class. They are still too 'rich' to benefit from the aid programmes, but too poor to be able to afford health insurance. Among them are also the unemployed who lost their insurance coverage with their jobs.

A kind of field hospital has pitched its tents here under the direction of the aid organization Remote Area Medical (RAM). Hundreds of volunteers, doctors, medical assistants, nurses and care workers are treating a steady stream of people who cannot afford a doctor – this in the United States, one of the richest and poorest countries in the world.

In the interview, Stan Brock, who founded RAM in 1985, explains: 'We are combating the underdevelopment of medical care. Twenty years ago we were in Mexico and Guatemala. Today two-thirds of our expeditions are in the United States.' And in this country, in which almost fifty million people are without health insurance, President Obama, who wants to remedy this scourge, is demonized as a 'new Hitler'. I can't get my head around this. One thing is certain: global domestic politics is bringing people closer together – and their lack of understanding for each other is growing.

The European policy of the national constitutional judges

In Germany, like in all other EU member states, the parliamentary authorities have passed the EU Treaty.

Thanks to the hard-fought struggle of Chancellor Angela Merkel, this treaty is supposed to ensure that the European Union can act both internally and externally in view of the enormous increase in the number of member states. In so doing, the democratic institutions in Germany – the Federal Government, the Bundestag and the Bundesrat – are performing the task laid down in the preamble to the German constitution to make Europe the guiding star of German politics. This democratic acceptance of the Lisbon Treaty is being challenged before the Federal Constitutional Court. And instead of bowing down in their red robes before democracy and declaring this matter (which has been decided in conformity with all of the rules of democracy) to be outside their jurisdiction (as they have often done in the past in similar cases), this time the constitutional judges are laying claim to an area of global domestic politics and passing judgement on democracy in Europe. It is remarkable that so much decision-making power should devolve to the subpolitics of national constitutional judges under certain conditions (namely, the complex relations of dependence between national and European law and the unanimity rule which dictates that all member states must approve the Treaty of Lisbon). The commentators in the German newspapers quickly concluded that the Federal Constitutional Court's Lisbon decision reinforces the rights of the German parliament in the process of European unification. Little attention was paid to the voices in France and other EU countries warning that in this way the German judges could unilaterally restrict the process of Europeanization, or even bring it to a halt. In fact, it would be hard to find a more striking example of how the national vision, which originated in and remains captive to the nineteenth century, fails to understand not only the reality of Europeanization but also the letter and spirit of the German constitution and German constitutional history.

The decisive norm appealed to by the judges (Art. 79 (3) Basic Law) does in fact set limits to constitutional amendments. It states that the democratic order may not abolish itself. This norm is the answer to the seizure of power in Germany by the National Socialists. What was conceived as a barrier against totalitarianism is now being used by the constitutional judges to place restrictions on the constitutional task of promoting European unification. For they are dictating to the democratic organs how they should in future deal with the claims of the EU: 'Either, dear Parliament, you disempower yourself and suspend the Basic Law by referendum – or the next time we will stop European integration!'

Clearly, the fact that in the meantime a European parliament exists which is democratically legitimized and also exercises control over the process of unification has entirely escaped the notice of these judges in their own case. They, the judges, who were elected by nobody, are the ones who are dictating to the parliament what a parliament is and should do.

The decision of the constitutional judges not only has a European – and hence also a global domestic political – dimension far beyond Germany, their area of jurisdiction. For it plays the nation state model of democracy off against Europeanization. By contrast, the great Europeans among the German politicians, from Konrad Adenauer to Willy Brandt and Helmut Kohl, always emphasized that the still incomplete German unity and the likewise still incomplete European integration are 'two sides of the same coin'. It is a paradoxical fact of contemporary history that, at the very moment when the pressure of the new global problems impinging on everyday life – ranging from the financial crisis through climate change to transnational networks of terrorism and drug trafficking – is compelling nation-states everywhere to form alliances in order to find practicable answers, the German constitutional court, of all institutions, is 'once again feeling the pinch of the German shoe', as Heinrich Heine already put it ironically 150 years ago.

What French President Mitterrand and German Chancellor Kohl hoped to achieve through the introduction of the monetary union – namely, to make European integration 'irreversible' – is being frivolously placed in jeopardy by the German constitutional judges. For Europe is one thing above all: Europeanization, thus a process that cannot be simply stopped without bringing about the disintegration of Europe. If this 'German spirit' prevails in Europe – following the slogan: 'Back to small state particularism under the banner "Rescue democracy!"' – then the British exception will become the European norm: back to the deluxe free-trade zone.

In global domestic politics, the coordination requirements that must be satisfied by European politics are also growing. If Europe does not want to be more than it is, if it persists in its incompatible energy policies, its incompatible fiscal policies and its incompatible social policies, then these policies will blow European integration apart from within at the next opportunity. Then the new Eastern European member states, which are still celebrating their recovered sovereignty, will soon cease to see any point in again having to recover and reinforce their sovereignty in the context of rule-governed European cooperation.

With all of this in mind, one must ask in all seriousness: who will protect Europe and Germany from these constitutional judges? Hopefully the parliament!

4

Harm in Exchange for Money

October 2009

Are we at war? Are we at peace? 'German soldiers order bombing raids' was the shocking news at the beginning of September. After the death of six Italian soldiers, the government in Rome is now also quarrelling over the withdrawal from Afghanistan. Precisely because this is disrupting or destroying the 'felt peace' in Europe, that is unlikely to be the last piece of bad news. With this, the question finally belongs to the order of business: what are Italian, German, British, French and American soldiers – and, not to forget, countless Afghani civilians! – dying for in Afghanistan in 2009? For the defence of the security interests of European countries in the Hindu Kush? For 'Never again 9/11'? For the conquest and subjugation of Afghanistan by NATO troops? For the imposition of capitalism and market freedom? For the democratization of the country? For victory over the Taliban who oppose women's rights as the work of the devil? No, it is more a matter of a paradigm shift with regard to the military option. What is at stake is the question of how it is possible under conditions of a self-endangering civilization, and hence of the irreversibility of global domestic politics, to combat or minimize global risks which pose an existential threat to everyone but can no longer be clearly identified and localized, in a 'preventive' way – that is, without civilization first having to collapse.

What is new is that, in the case of global risks in general, the compensation principle – harm in exchange for money – which permits, even normalizes, the limited (car) accident, fails and has to be replaced by the imperative of prevention or precaution. If man-made climate change has gone beyond the point of no return, if terrorists have access to atomic weapons, if the global economy has already imploded, then every measure comes too late! Therefore, we have to invest in new technologies, develop new notions of justice, reduce our consumption and pump billions into failing banks in order to prevent 'the worst', which must never occur and in the face of which our concepts fail. The fact has not yet really sunk in that a 'risk prevention war' is now also being conducted in Afghanistan in accordance with the same logic – prevention through war! Or to put it in more extreme and paradoxical terms: war on war! – and that as a result the clear boundaries between war and peace, enemy and friend, military and community service, were annulled.

None of those responsible wants to use the word 'war', because 'war' means war between states. And as a matter of fact it is not a war in this sense. NATO doesn't want to conquer Afghanistan but to help it onto its feet so that the country can defend itself and build democratic institutions and fill them with life. It is not doing this out of altruism and as an end in itself, however, but as a means to the end of banishing the risk of terrorism. Accordingly, the use of military force is spoken of in angelic pacifist terms and what is occurring is described in antiseptic Orwellian terms: 'peace mission', 'humanitarian intervention', 'military humanism', 'military operations other than war', 'warlike conditions'.

It was no less a figure than Carl von Clausewitz who, in his classic work *On War*, evoked the historicity of war. According to this view, every era has its own way of conducting war and as a result needs its own historical theory and contemporary diagnosis of war. Let me try to depict the difference between this type of war in the world risk society and its predecessors in other eras in very broad strokes. As Clausewitz shows, the understanding of war in the eighteenth century was founded on the balance between military powers and as such reflected the Newtonian fascination with mechanical structures and institutions characteristic of that period. By contrast, during the Cold War, overshadowed by the possible mutual self-destruction of the atomic powers, the imperative of prevention was introduced in the sense that the anticipation of the human disaster and its prevention became the maxim of the defence policy of the day. On the other hand, at that time two clearly identifiable and in principle predictable major powers confronted each other in the guise of NATO and the Warsaw Pact. Now that the Cold War is over and the bipolar world order has collapsed, the place of concretely identifiable actors and their military potential is being taken by the new indistinctness and unpredictability of anticipated catastrophes that have to be prevented at all costs:

> – The danger is acquiring new social dimensions; the military is targeting failed states, that is, non-state actors and shadowy networks which are potential sources of attacks; with this the separation between enemy and friend, soldier and civilian and war and peace is becoming blurred.

> – Threats are acquiring new spatial dimensions; this is true of climate change and its impacts as much as it is of breakdowns in the world economic system; but terrorism is also becoming globalized and is using the new means of transportation and communication (Internet, e-mail, flows of people, electronic money transactions, etc.) to organize itself.

– Finally, the danger is also spreading to new areas; global risks are becoming hydra-headed, including transnational terrorism, the proliferation of weapons of mass destruction, climate changes leading to outbreaks of violence and flows of climate refugees, though also the impacts of breakdowns of the global economy, and so on, and so forth. Many threats are not direct, intentional or certain, but indirect, unintentional and uncertain. In this way events which are at first sight remote are becoming possible events and potentially transnationally interlocking catastrophes are becoming the 'preventive' point of intervention and attack for military interventions. The aim is to minimize the – in a variety of senses – 'boundless' security risks in a 'post-heroic' way.

On the one hand, what is at stake in Afghanistan is in this sense the creation on foreign territory of a democratic order rooted in civil society, something which is evidently impossible without the consent and active involvement of the native population. This new hybrid of military force and Amnesty International creates and defends the liberal democratic, cosmopolitan order on the territory of other states, albeit against the resistance of the parties to the conflict, both of which at times violate human rights without scruple. (In Afghanistan, sections of the military and the police are also regarded as corrupt.) Thus, NATO is performing police functions in military disguise in global domestic politics. To castigate this as a violation of international law (as parties on the right and the left of the political spectrum are doing) is not only blind to history but more than anything fails to recognize the interdependencies and obligations generated by global domestic politics.

On the other hand, however, the attempt is being made to control global risks by military means, a dubious, treacherous dynamic full of innuendos: the risk is both real and non-existent, both present and absent, is uncertain and yet turns states into 'terror states' with apparent certainty. Ultimately risk can be assumed to be ubiquitous and thus it justifies a militarization of thought and action under the spell of the imperative of prevention based on the paradoxical, indeed counter-productive, calculation: a well-aimed military strike today spares the world an atomic disaster tomorrow – war on nuclear war!

The political magic of numbers

World rescue plans have become common answers to the shock on the financial markets. Everyone is carrying one or more around with him in his heart or maybe even in his coat pocket. This raises urgent questions about procedures, power and legitimation: who can enforce the measures which should now finally be taken? Against whom? And who should or should not be involved in this and why? Do Bavaria and Cameroon have to have voting rights here? Or is it enough if the USA and China – the 'G-2'! – negotiate everything among themselves and the others (e.g. the Europeans) give their assent – voluntarily, of course?

After Pittsburgh, many people are hoping that the G-20 could make the rising powers of the East and the South into co-creators of a new global order to be worked out. What many people have in mind might be called a kind of 'Metternich solution', a globalized Congress of Vienna, as it were; US Americans and Asians, Europeans and Africans, Latin Americans and Russians finally all come together to impose, for example, an internationally binding tax on the financial markets which is beneficial to all states in the teeth of the fierce opposition of the organized irresponsibility of speculative finance.

This undertaking is in danger of tripping over embarrassing little stumbling blocks, however. After all, there is the simple question of who should belong to the circle of the G-20 and who should not. Only the national heads of government? Or also the leaders of certain international organizations? Which ones? Including the EU? And then there is also the UN. (We had almost forgotten about it.) The problem is not only a numerical one. Behind it lurk questions of power, effectiveness and democracy: what does the new G-20 group 'stand' for?

No doubt it stands for the still indistinct, post-Western power constellation after the global economic crisis. How should it be located, with its competences and perspectives, its composition and authority, among the already existing fora and organizations whose goal is to bring about a cooperative consensus? How is the number 20 legitimized? Democratically? Surely not. Nobody is planning to hold elections on who should belong to the select group of G-20 states. Should, as is presently the case, the *de facto* standard of global economic power also be decisive under conditions of a normatively justified global domestic politics? Then what happens with the catastrophe-plagued poor countries who have contributed the least to the financial crisis and to climate change but are the most seriously affected by both? Will their fate then be sealed by a twofold exclusion?

Some people fear that the G-20 is undermining the already existing G-8 group of the leading industrial nations. Others think that a G-13 group (the G-8 plus the five largest emerging nations) might be a much more effective global forum. It is tempting to scoff at this political magic of numbers. In fact, however, this wrangling over the magical number that could establish consensus and legitimation within global domestic politics is a perfect metaphor for the residual hope of a world staring into the abyss.

In spite of all of their declarations of open-mindedness, the wealthy countries exhibit scant willingness to surrender their power within the institutions which they created in the middle of the last century to promote consensus and legitimacy. The emerging powers – especially, but not only, China and India – ask why they should collaborate in a system of balances if they do not occupy positions of power within it. And in point of fact: why do the Benelux countries still have more votes in the International Monetary Fund (IMF) than China? Yet the hesitation and reservations are not only on the side of the old powers. Isn't China laying claim to world power without responsibility? Doesn't it want to benefit from a new global order without having to shoulder the burdens of implementing and maintaining it? Does China have answers to the questions of 'why?' and 'where to?'? Something similar holds for India: isn't its willingness to share the costs of the rise of the global market severely hampered by the narrow definition of national interests to which the country and its government feel beholden?

When was the last time that a large number of countries even managed to agree on a concerted international response to a problem generally accepted as urgent? The last time that happened was fifteen years ago. In 1994, 123 countries came together to negotiate the creation of the World Trade Organization and they reached and implemented an agreement that laid down the basic rules of international trade. Since then, however, all attempts to reach a global trade agreement have consistently broken down. Something similar can be said about the cherished 'multilateralism' with regard to nuclear disarmament; the last important agreement was established in 1995, when 185 countries agreed to extend the existing non-proliferation treaty. Over the past fifteen years, however, India, Pakistan and North Korea have demonstrated that they have no intention of surrendering their status as nuclear powers.

In the spirit of cosmopolitan realism, it would make sense to adopt a 'minilateralism' (Moisés Naín). This would mean placing restrictions on the number of participants in order to finally come to grips with the major and minor global problems (e.g. the implementation of a global tax on financial speculation). The search for the magic number would then mean inviting the smallest number of countries possible to the negotiating table in order to maximize the probability of an enforceable regulation. Even this minilateral approach gives rise to injustices. For the least developed and often most seriously affected countries would once again be excluded from power. But the cosmopolitan touch, the realist magic, could be that minilateralism might be of greater help to everyone than multilateral wishful thinking.

So 'G-2' after all? Would that mean that we bow to the ubiquitous alternative: either survival or democracy?

5

Illegal World Citizens

November 2009

The 2000 *sans papiers* (undocumented migrants) who have taken up residence in a vacant department store in the centre of Paris, Rue Baudelique 14, in the 18th arrondissement, are not concealing themselves. On the contrary, these West Africans, Turks, Pakistanis, Chinese, etc., are doing everything in their power to draw attention to their lack of rights and to their whereabouts. Every Wednesday, the 'protest march of the *sans papiers*' takes to the streets with rousing banners and hands out leaflets. It is a play of power(lessness) in which people without rights – in France they are neither called nor are they lawbreakers but plain 'undocumented': '*sans-papiers*' (the correct official term is '*étrangers en situation irrégulière*' – foreigners in an irregular situation); in England, the similar, but drier, term is 'undocumented workers', in Italy '*clandestini*' (stowaways); in Germany, however, they are harshly called 'illegal immigrants', verbally anticipating the practice of expulsion – play their hopeless situation out against the contradictions in which the overwhelming power of the Western countries has trapped them. The wealthy democracies are carrying the banner of equality and human rights into the farthest corners of the earth without noticing that, in so doing, the legitimacy of the national border fortresses with which they want to repel the flows of migrants is being undermined. The migrants in Paris take the proclaimed human right to mobility seriously and courageously bring it to bear against their functional exploitation in the wealthy countries and states which, precisely in the light of increasing internal inequalities, want the proclaimed norm of equality to end at their militarized borders.

What would be unthinkable in an Italy running verbal riot against the *clandestini*, though also in Germany and Hungary, and indeed in many countries throughout the world, is not at all uncommon in France. Here the undocumented workers actually go on strike on occasion (even successfully) with the aim of pressurizing their employers into procuring residence and work permits for them. And in recent years migrants have repeatedly occupied French churches, government offices and universities and in non-violent sit-down strikes refused to leave them before they were 'legalized'. However, the camp of illegal immigrants in the Rue Baudelique is unparalleled both in scope and in visibility. Yet, the government of the hyperactive immigration sceptic Sarkozy has made no move to clear it. Why? How should this be understood?

The *sans papiers* are a severe embarrassment for the French government. On the one hand, many French people are calling for even more severe restrictions to at least curb the flows of illegal migrants. On the other hand, a concerted use of police force by the government against the *sans papiers* would be met with historically grounded public resistance. The French still proudly regard their nation as the birthplace of human rights. A not unimportant point is also that in France, unlike Germany and Italy, the major unions have embraced the cause of the *sans papiers* and have inscribed it on the banners of the proud tradition of workers' struggles.

It is hardly surprising, therefore, that the organizer of the *sans papiers* movement (who himself emigrated illegally from Senegal to France in 1999 and in 2003 acquired the 'papers' that make people into human beings) is a guest in a regular morning radio programme broadcast under the title 'The voice of the *sans papiers*.' When asked why the immigrants who have ensconced themselves in the department store have not been encircled by the police and led away, he cannot suppress a giggle. 'That is actually a bit surprising', he acknowledges. But paradoxically it is precisely their visibility that protects them. 'Mass arrests? The French wouldn't put up with that. And the government knows it.'

The system needs 'illegals'

What is actually behind the label 'illegal immigrants'? It refers to people who in all of the wealthy, and increasingly also the developing, regions of the world (hence Southeast Asia, for example) take on jobs that nobody else in these countries wants to do – building services, menial jobs in hotels, restaurants and their kitchens, caring for the elderly and children in the private homes of the up-and-coming middle class. The *sans papiers* of the world have to work undercover, and thus for low wages of between six and eight euros per hour, according to those living in the Rue Baudelique; others work under the names of legal friends. They claim that a majority of them even pay taxes and that they are also subject to automatic social security deductions (for healthcare and retirement), even though they will never be able to claim the corresponding benefits. 'Illegality' makes these mobile citizens of the world vulnerable to blackmail and exploitation. They are devoid of rights. But their activities and services are functionally necessary, for their own survival and – across borders – for that of their families of origin, but above all also for the survival of the affluent Western countries and of the emerging countries. One can and must feel moral outrage over the desperate situation of human beings who only want to work hard to support their families and most of whom are compelled to live a hyper-conformist existence in the European countries because they have to be permanently on their guard, often over decades, to avoid any conspicuousness. But that is not the point.

The point is rather that the boastful humanity of the West at its core presupposes inhumanity in dealings with the 'illegals'! Without their active presence, without their bad pay, which is closely related to their lack of rights, without the self-sacrificing assistance they provide in caring for the elderly and in minding children in private homes struggling to strike a balance between the rights of men and women, whole societies would collapse. In a word, illegals are 'necessary for the system', just as are the large banks or the courts which condemn them. We deceive ourselves about this with the category of 'illegals'. This blanket, anticipatory criminalization obscures the functional indispensability of their services for us while mobilizing the moral outrage and legal condemnation in advance which lower the price of labour power and facilitate their exploitation. The good conscience about this is thrown in gratis, as it were, provided free of charge along with the criminalization!

In Italy, the Berlusconi government has topped it all. Here anyone who knows about illegal immigrants (perhaps a doctor treating them free of charge or a schoolteacher teaching their children) and does not report them to the authorities is subject to punishment. Hannah Arendt spoke of the 'stateless people' who had acquired the status of the medieval 'outlaws' in the modern world. What she was not yet able to see is how modern capitalism and the global hierarchical division of labour between poor and rich countries and pop-ulations which it creates and exploits has itself revived a 'labour market of outlaws' in the centres of the Western constitutional states and has given rise to its contradictory transnational institutionalization.

That is a kind of global domestic politics which is unfolding equally at the macro and the micro levels, at the centres of private happiness and the promised equality, that is, in families. The emancipation compromise in dual income households with an aspiration to gender equality is tacitly based on this 'organized illegality', the quiet assistance of *sans papiers*, undocumented workers, *clandestini* and illegal immigrants from the impoverished regions of the world. One could call them 'peace-keeping forces' in the battle of the sexes. Nobody wants to know about this exactly, even though everyone is quite well aware of it. For, to repeat, the system is illegal – and that's why it works. A prime example of this is care of the elderly. Those in need of care and their relations have hardly any chance to act really legally. Hungarian or Polish geriatric nurses earn around 1,200 euros per month in German families. They get room and board for free. This is a lot of money for the patients and their families – on the one hand. On the other, though, it is also very little. For this, the nurses are often on call around the clock; and if one compares their earnings with the costs for a German nursing service, they are a 'bargain': a German nursing service would charge at least 8,000 euros. The dilemma faced by the relatives is evident. At times of shrinking incomes, in particular, they can choose between two ways of making themselves liable to prosecution: either they hire an illegal nurse or they make themselves liable to prosecution for failing to provide assistance to a father or a mother.

P.S.: Who actually looks after the children, the old and the sick in the poorer countries of origin of the mothers who, serving as outlaws in our countries, make possible the armistice (it would be an exaggeration to speak of 'peace' in this regard) in the battle of the sexes?

Human genetic eugenics?

In a world in which all kinds of risks that permeate the public and private spheres and torment and fascinate people are ubiquitous, there are many reasons for seeking refuge in an 'outside', in a world beyond risk. However, an essential consequence of the globality of risks in particular (as climate change and the financial crisis have made palpable) is the emergence of a common world, a world which we share come what may, a world for which there is no 'outside', no 'exit', no 'other' any longer.

Global domestic politics means: no matter how congenial or strange people of different skin colour, nationality and origin may appear to us, in order to survive we have to coexist and cooperate with these 'alien others' in this world of corruption, suffering and exploitation. One conclusion says: bury all values of 'political purity' that delude you into thinking that you do not belong, that you are an outsider! Another conclusion is that the heightened awareness of global risks also opens up spaces for alternative conceptions of the future, indeed for alternative modernities! Global risks are destabilizing the self-destructive banking system and climate-changing industrial systems. As a result, they can be seen as a vitally important step towards constructing new institutions and prompt calls for political action throughout the world. Moreover, faced with unavoidable risks, we confront the challenge of developing a 'cosmopolitan outlook'. Are global risks calculable from a cosmopolitan perspective? No, because their existence or non-existence depend essentially on cultural perceptions, evaluations and decisions which can assume radically contrasting forms depending on historical experiences.

There can be no better illustration of this than the dramatic implications of biomedicine, in particular in the areas of reproductive medicine, prenatal diagnostics and stem cell research, including the cloning of human beings. Were one to identify two global opposite poles of cultural evaluation and decision here, they would be represented by Israel and Germany. Israel goes further than any other country in the area of biomedicine. The aim is to ensure the survival of the nation through a high birth rate. What is hotly debated, or even prohibited, in Germany, is accepted and practised here. Thus Israel permits surrogate motherhood provided that a committee that must be consulted by law has given its assent to the agreement. Decisive for this, however, is that the egg donor mothers must be Jewish, a requirement strictly monitored by the Orthodox authorities. Israel's sperm banks are also open to single women and lesbians. If a man dies, for example, in an accident, sperm may be extracted from him *post mortem* so that his wife can have herself fertilized. It has also become quite common for soldiers to donate their sperm before going to war. Should they be killed, the parents can look for a surrogate mother and with her aid bring the much longed-for grandchild into the world.

Pre-implantation diagnostics (PID), through which embryos are examined for genetic defects in the test tube prior to implementation and excluded if any are found, is a routine procedure in Israel. The country also holds the world record for genetic tests prior to and during pregnancy – fourteen are usual in the case of non-Orthodox women. Even minor deviations from the norm often lead to an abortion, sometimes even a cleft lip and palate revealed by ultrasound.

Almost everything which is permitted largely without conflict in Israel is controversial or prohibited in Germany. The key point is that both Israelis and Germans appeal to the Holocaust! However, Jews were its victims, whereas Germans were the perpetrators.

The strict moral guidelines of German bioethics are influenced by the Nuremberg Trials in which Nazi doctors had to answer for their crimes against Jews and other groups. As a result, the concept 'eugenics' is highly charged in Germany, but not in Israel. Zionism and eugenics are not mutually exclusive but complement each other. The Zionists celebrated the image of the healthy and strong 'muscular Jew' as a contrasting image to the oppressed diaspora Jew. This desire for a 'better human being' lives on in the liberal practice in biomedicine.

To generalize, the complications and confusions of global domestic politics are exacerbated by the fact that all risks are not equal. For some they open up possibilities (hence the door to progress) whose exploitation represents a crime for others.

6

The Cards of Power Are Being Reshuffled across the World

December 2009

General Motors, only a year ago a dinosaur threatened by extinction, has risen like a phoenix from the ashes of bankruptcy. As an expression of new strength, the company management has suddenly reversed itself and announced that it doesn't want to sell Opel, the 'European branch', after all, even though the sale seemed to have been long since finalized.

Suddenly the political cartographers have to perform herculean labour because the power landscapes of global domestic politics, which on this occasion were laid bare by eruptions and landslides, have to be re-surveyed. For many decades, just a few coordinates – left/right, us/them, national/international – provided sufficient political orientation. 'Operation Opel', however, discharged tensions created by tectonic shifts. Suddenly it is becoming apparent that the still entirely unexplored continent of global domestic politics is forcing so many actors with the most diverse backgrounds and interests together across all borders that one can already imagine the scope of the doctoral theses which may one day be written about them. Among the characters in this play are: a US president and numerous European heads of government; commissioners in Brussels and German state prime ministers; in the case of the German government, first the big coalition with key figures from the three parties the CDU, the CSU and the SPD, and now a small coalition, again with three parties; a disappointed prospective buyer from Italy; and a Canadian-Austrian-Russian would-be winner who cannot believe that its winning bid is no longer valid after all. And let us not forget the tens of thousands of employees and their union representatives in the various Opel production sites across Europe, who, like deer caught in the headlamps of globalization, are engaged in fierce competitive struggles.

Global domestic politics is defined in the first instance, therefore, by the fact that powerbrokers and spheres of influence that seemed to be forever outside are now inside, while national boundaries and institutions continue to exist. The cards of power are being reshuffled across the world. The arena is de-territorialized; the confrontations are occurring simultaneously here and elsewhere. So many flags are flying on the virtual battlefields of global domestic politics that the commanders seem to have long since lost any overview.

Global domestic politics and global economic policy

Where but a short time ago clear boundaries still existed between spheres of influence and power blocs (state and economy, USA and EU, government and opposition), no-man's-lands are suddenly opening up. Major flows of power branch off into rivulets and then swell up abruptly once again. Some governments – for example, the German – entertained the belief that they could reorganize the global automobile industry through a mammoth global domestic political coalition. That humanity must be saved from the impending climatic disaster was suddenly forgotten; the interests of all human beings are now being egoistically elbowed aside (not to say into the abyss). The hope has already evaporated that the Chinese would learn the lesson from the disastrous energy record of the automobile-infatuated West and renounce the dream of a car of one's own.

The political atlases of the past decades now have only archival value in view of the global shifts that the Opel debacle brought to light. The global financial and banking crisis, though also the automobile crisis and the attacks by transnational terrorist networks, were celebrated as 'the hour of the state'. Does that still hold? Or are the dormant volcanoes again becoming active so that, following state socialism for the rich, we are now experiencing the counter-revolution of the managers? Hasn't the socialization of the losses by the state given rise to the paradox that the banks and companies which are 'necessary for the system' can reassert themselves now that they have been freed from the risk of collapse? For they are selling off the jobs in a worldwide auction to those states offering the highest subventions. The Opel management emphatically denies this, of course, but the strategic power situation (the competition among the European Opel production sites and the political importance of jobs) speaks for itself.

Accordingly, the decision by General Motors not to sell Opel has prompted very different reactions at the Opel production sites. Whereas people in Kaiserslautern and Antwerp are worried about thousands of job losses, those affected in Great Britain, Spain and Poland seem to be comparatively content. There they think they have a strong hand should new austerity measures soon be announced in the corporate head office in Detroit.

Viewed from the perspective of mobile capital, therefore, a form of state power exhibiting the following characteristics of a 'national global market state' is 'ideal':

– The state must be easily replaceable and interchangeable;

– it must find itself in competition with the largest possible number of states of the same kind (for example, for jobs);

– it must have internalized the neoliberal global market regime, in particular open borders for goods and capital (not, by contrast, for labour and workers).

– The state must impose this global market regime domestically as 'reform policy' and work towards its realization at the global level; and finally

– the state should cultivate the national because the emphasis on national sovereignty perpetuates competition between states; at the same time, this enduringly frustrates to the discovery and development of the political added value that states acquire from cooperation geared to regulating global markets.

Germany, for example, benefits enormously from European cooperation and from the fact that national borders have been opened up. Very few states are as reliant on international trade as the export world champion. Nevertheless, the Opel case is bringing a nationalism to light at the highest political level which was believed to have been long since overcome: 'No Opel euros to America!' demand the politicians. That is the national reflex which is blind and makes us blind to the power opportunities within global domestic politics that each individual state gains from the merging of states.

An actor called humanity

But will we ever be able to trust 'Mr Market' again? Or the economists? Or democracy? Or the law? Because the dirty little secret is that all of the things which are plunging the world into the abyss are legal. Everything which is threatening or wreaking havoc today was set in train by national governments in cooperation with relevant groups of experts and with the blessing of democracy. This holds as much for the climate catastrophe as for the financial crash.

In this respect, realistic political answers to these challenges presuppose a highly improbable transformation in the self-understanding of the West. Hitherto, the affluent West regarded itself as the model for the world; now it is forced to recognize that it developed a doomsday model and made it the foundation of its global modernization mission. This has momentous consequences for climate policy, for example. If the Chinese and Indians will not cooperate anyway, one often hears, why should the industrial countries support any agreements at all? Yet such a negotiation tactic misjudges and denies the historical background of the new global inequalities which are taking hold. First forcing the emerging countries to make concessions only later to reward them with concessions is doomed to failure.

Give and take can only succeed the other way around: the rich countries must front up and then the poor of the world will give their consent. The end effect may be the same but the perspective on the problem is the opposite. This approach makes the situation and outlook of the most seriously affected countries its own and implies the insight that the industrial countries are primarily responsible for the world's problems and hence have a greater responsibility for solving them. To this must also be added that they possess substantially larger resources for solving these problems, and indeed may even benefit greatly from solving them through the export of 'clean' technologies.

For what is ultimately at stake is not only the reduction of emissions, CO_2 certificates and the world-wide implementation of solar and wind generation technology and other achievements of climate diplomacy. In the end it is a question of how the political force that flows from the insight into the man-made collective threat can be used to place an actor called humanity, a subject capable of responding to these problems, on a firm political footing.

Hence, the struggle over climate and financial policy is ultimately a struggle to reinvent and refound the political in a way which corrects the system of national sovereignty as it was worked out and established in the West through a cosmopolitan global domestic political legal order which simultaneously binds the nation states and is implemented by them jointly in the face of resistance. Nobody knows whether this can be successful. But this much is clear: the 'cosmopolitical imperative' – 'cooperate or bust!' – holds everywhere.

Three scenarios for a future global domestic politics can be derived from this: an optimistic, a realistic, and a pessimistic one. The optimistic scenario states that, just as the fragmented plurality of small-scale systems of government was successfully transformed into national imagined communities (Benedict Anderson) during the nineteenth century, it may be possible, in view of the progressing self-destruction of civilization, to create imagined cosmopolitan communities at the beginning of the twentieth century. These should not negate the national identities and states, for example, but should instead reconfigure them into a new type of sovereignty through cosmopolitan openness and cooperation. The EU is the historical example of this.

According to the realistic scenario, the climate change agnostics will retain the upper hand; an eco-technological business-as-usual modernization and a more or less 'green capitalism' will develop; the more openly the mainstream political parties agree in this sense in their desire to keep the large tankers on course, the greater, more absurd and more implausible their staged antagonisms become (not only during election campaigns). This is the classical position of Niklas Luhmann: evolution is sufficient, change is not an option

– therefore, one should try to minimize the damage caused by excitement! Silence detoxifies!

The third, negative scenario is by no means incompatible with this mainstream position, and may even be a consequence of it. Given that global domestic politics is irreversible, the radically unequal consequences of climate change and of climate policy (and of globalization in general) will 'fan the flames' of fundamentalist counter-movements. In other words, the outcome will be an ominous vicious circle of climate catastrophes, flows of migrants, fundamentalist nationalism and religious fundamentalism as well as outbreaks of violence (climate wars). As empirical studies show, corresponding trends within regions which have followed completely different paths in the modern era are already extremely pronounced.

Are we therefore experiencing the autumn of national politics? The commentaries in the newspapers are falling on the parties like wilted leaves; the opinion polls have a musty smell of political and electoral abstinence; the German federal elections were a dull reflection of summer days of democracy long past. It has been decades since so terribly much has been consistently written on the weaknesses, mistakes and infirmities of the political parties.

But it is by no means politics as such that is being buried. Elections are being held as before. They decide who is the winner and the loser, who gets to govern and who allocates the offices, and hence who has the say – even if there is nothing to say. What is being buried is only the ability of politics to shape events, the expectation that politics can find answers to the problems preying on people's minds throughout the world. But what is meant by 'only' here? What is being buried is the claim of politics to be politics, that is, to shape the present and future of societies.

In the era of global domestic politics, the substantive political questions have moved beyond the horizon of the nation state. The associated quantum leap is defined precisely by the fact that the historical logic of electing and being elected has become uncoupled from the still-to-be-comprehended logic of precautionary and preventive political action in a self-endangering civilization. The questions of what politics can shape and the questions of electability belong to different centuries, so to speak.

Accordingly, intellectual debates are being conducted over whether politics 'must', 'should' or 'can' undergo a global domestic political turn without national electability; at the same time, the profane maxims of power and feasibility of national electability without the promise of being able to shape global domestic policy are proving their worth as a good electoral strategy and hence are setting the trend.

The upshot is that the power to shape events is staged but political action is actually oriented to maximizing votes. Electability without the prospect of shaping events, the vision to shape events without electoral prospects – this is at the core of the disenchantment with politics among the voters, though also among the politicians. In the process, normal democracy is in danger of degenerating into formal democracy in which the major, passionate questions of global domestic politics never become the object of everyday politics but remain the adornments of soapbox oratory.

Everywhere the questions of the 'why?' and the 'whither?' of modernity are being posed in a new form: if the political realism which remains caught up in the national outlook is becoming false, what power rules govern global domestic politics? Who speaks for nature and how does this voice acquire the power to prevail? What kind of social justice makes sense in the twenty-first century? What role do immigrants, these illegal citizens of the world, play in this connection? What role is played by the global subpolitics of reproductive medicine, genetic engineering, nanotechnology, biotechnology, and so on?

In earlier times, German elections actually turned on substantive issues: alignment with the West (Adenauer), the economic miracle (Erhard), *Ostpolitik* (Brandt) and unification (Kohl), to mention just the themes which polarized and mobilized politics in Germany. In global domestic politics the primacy of politics can be recovered only if national politics becomes European. 'Social Europe', 'environmental Europe' – these would be major substantive policy issues with the potential to trigger polarizing mobilizations in national domains. Or, to put it in general terms: substantive policy either assumes transnational and cooperative forms – or does not occur at all.

7

Felt Peace and Waged War

January 2010

For forty years, everyday Germans hardly noticed that there was such a thing as a Bundeswehr. That remained true even when, in recent years, almost 200,000 young Germans were suddenly plunged into the turmoil of a decade in which international campaigns were waged against the global risk of terrorism.

Several thousand German soldiers are in the meantime serving in Afghanistan, Bosnia, Kosovo and the Democratic Republic of the Congo, off the coast of Lebanon and in the Horn of Africa, and as observers in Georgia, Eritrea and Sudan. Their missions have unwieldy names – Isaf, KFor, EUFor, Unifil, UNmee, and so forth – names which are as complicated as global domestic politics with all its messy conflicts, which the German soldiers are supposed to help resolve. Germany is also learning terms such as that of the 'asymmetrical war', which terrorists are waging against states and states against terrorists. Thus the idea of people being killed is gradually regaining its place in the German intellectual world – and now, following the Kunduz airstrike, also that of deliberate killing.

In Afghanistan we are dealing with the new type of 'virtual war' in global domestic politics or, to be more precise, with the socially constructed, selective virtuality of war across borders. With Baudrillard, one could say, to put it provocatively, that the war in Afghanistan is not even taking place. The weakness of his thesis is that the war is taking place.

The decisive point, however, is that both statements are true! The war is taking place. Over forty countries are taking part in it under US leadership. The global domestic political message read out of the debris of the World Trade Centre was that a country must never again become the refuge of globally operating terrorism. But this war had to be organized as 'felt peace'. This means that it had to take place 'elsewhere', 'for others', but not in the countries of the belligerent nations, and certainly not in and for Germany. Thus both the 'felt peace' and the 'waged war' exist concurrently and are interconnected. This constellation can remain relatively stable only as long as the felt peace and the actual war are spatially and socially separated from each other and are connected with each other in accordance with a specific pattern of staging and legitimation, namely, with the schema of the selective virtuality of war. (Incidentally, Baudrillard's hyperbole expresses the Western outlook, the outlook which is blind to the other side's casualties.)

However, this half-measure virtuality has to be expressly produced and maintained, both socially and politically. It puts the seal on the domestic invisibility of what the soldiers have to perform, accomplish, endure and suffer on a daily basis in foreign lands. Producing virtuality for domestic consumption while having to conduct a war to prevent war abroad gives rise to one contradiction after another, which demote every defence minister to a self-defence minister. For this can succeed only if the war is something which takes place 'over there', if the war dead are not 'our' dead, if German soldiers do not kill any civilians. This manufactured unreality of war requires an extreme hierarchy, namely, the decoupling of the place where the decisions are made from the country in which the 'side effects', the 'collateral damage' occur. Thus the dividing line between felt peace and waged war coincides exactly with the dividing line between virtuality and reality which has to be erected and maintained by the Western armed forces and governments.

This strategy of minimizing risk follows the risk aversion of the West. In societies in which killing for military purposes is tabooed and human rights enjoy priority the outbreak of armed violence is especially shocking. In past 'total' wars, the military imperative permeated all domains of social action. Governments were able to nationalize companies, control production, postpone elections and impose news censorship. The opposite holds for the virtual war. The risk can be redistributed only if the contradictions of militarism are restricted by offloading them onto the professional practice of the armed forces.

All of this renders the virtuality of war extremely fragile. The images and stories published in the mass media or circulated in the Internet constitute a central theatre of war because of their (de)legitimizing power. The Internet is becoming a dangerous field of activity for warring nations because secret information can decide over success and failure in virtual wars. It can bring about the collapse of the difference between waged war and felt peace. Informants and sources that use the Internet escape the control of the warring nations, however, and can reach and mobilize global public opinion because they operate transnationally. Because virtual wars are conducted under the eyes of the camera, there is no such thing as a purely military success. An action which strikes a particular military target but leaves behind moral and political debris has missed its target. No doubt this dependence of virtual war on the mass media represents a pacifying factor because it increases the political risks and costs even for the militarily powerful and most powerful countries.

Consequently, the Western media management strategy is directed less to imposing the official line and much more to at least ensuring that nothing happens which could jeopardize the virtuality of warfare. To be sure, a lot happens in wars which journalists and the general public find disturbing. Thus the extremity of war must almost always be concealed. Hence, the governments of Western countries certainly expect to meet with criticism and uncomfortable questions. What they fear most of all, however, is a single incident such as the one in Kunduz which is so grave that it could lead to the collapse of the established reporting because it brings home all too clearly to journalists, newspaper readers and television viewers the need for an entirely new perspective on things.

As long as the images of the suffering of the others do not sabotage the foundations of the official story as to the 'why?' of the war, they do not jeopardize the felt peace. This boundary was evidently breached by the cynical violence of the scornful and brutal images of torture from the US prison in Iraq and by the news reports emerging from the Guantanamo prison camp with its contempt for the Geneva Conventions and human rights. Both of these scandals destroyed the official legend because they showed the whole world that the US campaign against terrorism and for human rights dramatically flouts human rights.

The Kunduz incident is both similar and different for Germany. This much is clear: nobody, neither Defence Minister Guttenberg nor Chancellor Merkel, has presented the whole truth to the public to date. Again and again contradictory versions are finding their way into the public domain all of which inadvertently places the why-narrative in question. For didn't we believe that the German soldiers were not hunting Taliban but were instead training policemen and operating in something like the capacity of the military arm of Amnesty International? This is how the construction of the virtuality of the war in Afghanistan in global domestic politics is collapsing. War is returning to Germany. And not only the self-defence minister finds himself in severe difficulties.

When non-knowing rules

Reports are coming in from the United States that the swine flu has spread to chickens so that we must now anticipate an amalgamation of the swine flu and the avian flu virus. This raises the question: who is going to lose their head first: the pigs, the hens or the humans?

There can be no doubt that the swine-avian-human flu has long since become a global domestic political phenomenon. Anyone who thinks of nation states in terms of self-enclosed containers can neither understand this problem nor counteract it. To be sure, biomedical problems play a pivotal role. But equally important are worldwide mobility, goods traffic, media coverage, Internet communication and the national healthcare systems, the different levels of vulnerability of populations and population groups and the cultural perceptions in which this risk 'is' at times a terrifying menace, at others a nine days' wonder.

When America sneezes, the rest of the world arms itself for preventive measures against threats. In the meantime at least one in 200 Americans has been infected with the virus, in Great Britain there is one viral infection for every 300 persons. The World Health Organization, which is coordinating the information and the medical responses and preventive measures, states that in the meantime the illness has spread to over 180 countries and has led to the deaths of more than 4,000 persons. If one compares this (somewhat cynically) with the deaths on the road throughout the world to which we have become accustomed, then many people ask whether here hysteria is being produced and fomented (the ulterior motive being profits and jobs in the pharmaceutical industry); and many people are calling for a 'rational risk assessment' – finally!

However, on this occasion a secret must be disclosed: the scientific calculation of risk called for and then administered to anxious mothers and fathers as information in the mass media is often nothing more than an unacknowledged groping in the dark, dressed up in scientific jargon. Particularly when it comes to the globalized risk phenomena with which we have recently been increasingly confronted, non-knowing outweighs knowledge; reassurance is always drawn from the past, anxiety from the future. The course of the swine flu triggered by the H1N1 virus has been relatively harmless until now. But will the virus undergo a mutation and lead to a pandemic that will cost millions of human beings their lives? Nobody knows or is in a position to know this. This non-knowing is not the result of bad science but, on the contrary, is a by-product of more and better science. But in order to be able to act 'responsibly', we must act 'as if' we knew something.

Therefore calculating risk also involves risk. After all, it was precisely the unshakeable faith of the mathematical economists that they had once and for all mastered non-knowing with regard to risks that was an essential contributing factor to the financial catastrophe.

Given the quasi-awareness and acknowledgement of non-knowing, the pandemic risk permits just two (wrong) decisions: either one takes precautions, in which case one is accused of hysteria; or one does nothing, and then the complaint is: irresponsibility wherever one looks! That is symptomatic. The world of calculable and controllable risk releases an element of surprise (particularly in the light of the triumph of the claim to be able to master such risks) or, to be more precise, of manufactured uncertainties, in other words of the insecurities and uncertainties first created by the attempts to overcome them.

When John Maynard Keynes sought to unravel the secrets of economics in the 1930s after the first global economic crisis, his reflection ultimately turned on the irreversibility of the uncertainty that springs from the claim of mathematical models to overcome it. First there is the difference between model Platonism and reality. The model assumptions of the economic sciences are postulates that by no means necessarily coincide with the actual decisions and their consequences and side effects in economic, political and social reality. Keynes drew the conclusion that the prevailing economic doctrines were misleading and could lead to catastrophes if applied to the world of facts. In the idealized world of the mathematical economic sciences, it was generally accepted that fluctuations in the economic cycle are regrettable, transient phenomena and not phenomena inherent in an economic system founded on risk. One only needed to change some framework conditions which distort the free play of forces for risk to unfold its power to create boundless happiness. The economic well-being of all was just around the next corner, as it were. The fact that 'risk', by its very logic, means uncertainty – and not just negatively as potential catastrophes (collapse of the global economy, etc.), but also positively, as surprise and as a precondition of creativity – remains beyond the purview of this risk-model science.

Keynes already objected to this:

By 'uncertain' knowledge . . . I do not mean merely to distinguish what is known for certain from what is merely probable. The game of roulette is not subject, in this sense, to uncertainty . . . The sense in which I am using the term is that in which the prospect of a European war is uncertain, or the price of copper and the rate of interest twenty years hence . . . About these matters there is no scientific basis on which to form any calculable probability whatever. We simply do not know. (1937)

One is tempted to add: perhaps it is not even possible for us to know it. This simple, age-old and simultaneously alarming new insight expresses the anxiety of the age which has infected and permeated everything and everybody.

8

The Return of Social Darwinism or: Which University Do We Want?

February 2011

In the 1960s, Georg Picht and Ralf Dahrendorf proclaimed the 'educational catastrophe'. The answer was: education for all. The Bologna process has failed. As a result, a new educational catastrophe is looming: no education for all! Bologna was successful where two world wars had failed, namely, in destroying the universities in their traditional, successful sense.

An anti-education educational reform is firing off its plastic words – excellence, competence, efficiency, modularization, and so forth – without restraint and an in part cowed, in part sympathetic university administration and professoriate is translating them into reality. However, the self-delusion of the educational policy-makers is reflected in the insolence with which they must take their plastic language for reality itself. They say 'bachelor's degree' and launch the McDonaldization of the university. For 'fast food' read 'fast education'.

The modularization is leading to the dissolution of the expert standards in areas of discourse which evolved over decades. In the end, chronically understaffed institutes in the social sciences and the humanities are no longer able to offer their own degrees. The last remaining expert in each field switches out the light. In order to ensure that everything occurs in an orderly fashion, however, the state is developing a kind of McKinsey-Stalinism in the guise of networks of accreditors, evaluators, educational planners and educational spies. This is very close to an East Germanization of the Federal Republic. I propose that the students should award an annual 'Margot Honecker Prize' at their universities and at the national level for the most outstanding absurdity in the everyday insanity of educational policy. For it is the students, and they alone, who have demonstrated the initiative and courage to defend the idea of the university against the superior power of the reformers as sanctioned by the state.

According to an ironic retrospective observation since the 1960s the number of those who fought in the resistance against the Nazi regime has been growing on a daily basis. Since the unexpected successes of the student protests against a reform that requires them to put in sixty-hour working weeks, the number of professors and public commentators who opposed it 'from the beginning' has been growing daily. However, the newly inflamed debate is in danger of losing its way in the technical details of educational policy while the question concerning the alternative – Which university do we want? – is screened out. Here I would like to address this question in two steps: which historical change is convulsing higher education? And what role should the reformed university play in the changed world?

The national model of the university is in ruins

At Harvard, one can learn that the Humboldtian conception of education is more modern than ever. Almost all of the apparently eternal ways of mastering uncertainty – family, marriage, gender roles, classes, parties, churches and, finally, the welfare state – are losing importance. To date just three answers have been offered to this perfecting of uncertainty: education, education, education! And not: training, training, training! For, by taking one's orientation from the labour market, one turns 'economic need' into the point of reference which later may no longer exist in this form in the rapidly changing world of work.

It is not the university as such that lies in ruins but the national model of the university. The historical framework conditions under which the nation state and the modern concept of national culture give rise to each other are being washed away by an increasingly transnationalizing economy, culture, and politics. These developments are putting an end to the omnipotence of the state in education, to the elite character of the university (as regards both access and curriculum), to the legend of the academic ivory tower and, not least, to the 'methodological nationalism' of the university. What is meant by this?

Under the impression of the national unity of state and university, the humanities and social sciences have also 'quite naturally' become accustomed to conceptualizing and studying the state as a nation state, society as a national society, identity as national identity, history as national history, inequality as national equality, justice as national justice and democracy as national democracy. This conserves false paths in knowledge and education at a time when boundaries are becoming muddled and effaced by transnational developments, when the practical options in economics and politics are increasing, when new multinational forms of the family and careers in education and the working world are developing – in short, in the globalized world. Nothing exhibits this as clearly as the European reality in which the intermeshing of national societies and of nation states is simply incomprehensible in terms of methodological nationalism.

Humboldt II: The university as the school of world citizenship

Thus the universities are suffering the profane fate of other public service providers and institutions. And the answer calls for nothing less than a squaring of the circle. It has to reconcile contradictory goals, namely, the dictate of financial policy to do less and the dictate of democratic politics to do more (mass education and elite education). In coping with these difficulties, three programmatic options for educational policy can be distinguished. The advocates of the nostalgic agenda turn a blind eye to these historical changes and embrace the conservative motto: why should anything change in the fact that nothing changes (in particular if we play our part in ensuring that nothing changes)?

The second option in educational policy, the neoliberal agenda, sets about remodelling the university into a market university as though it were a marmalade factory. Those who work in marmalade factories need not be fond of marmalade. The global domestic political agenda differentiates itself from both positions. I distinguish between Humboldt I (nineteenth century) and Humboldt II (twenty-first century), where the latter represents a global domestic political agenda that strives to refound the idea of the university as a school of world citizenship.

The neoliberal fanatics are not short of justifications for the national educational policy of empty classrooms: the cheaper the education the better. Bachelor's degree equals reduction in the length of study, equals easing of public budgets. Whether those who graduate with a bachelor's degree find jobs is their own problem.

In the employment society shaped by industry, human beings were trained to be as perfect imitators of pre-given blueprints as possible. In an age of global competition, by contrast, creative cross-border commuters who are capable of acting autonomously, taking the initiative and demonstrating solidarity across borders are becoming more important both for the economy and for democratic society. The purpose of all universities, also and especially in the twenty-first century, is to sharpen one's own ideas through the confrontation with those of others. This does not follow from the idealism of the Enlightenment, however, but from the economic realism of the world economy. That is Humboldt II, not the proposals of McKinsey!

Reforms of the university in accordance with principles of the market appeal to the goals of doing away with the university founded on privileges and implementing the principle 'More opportunities for all.' However, the opposite is threatening to occur, namely, the return of social Darwinism under the pressure of globalization. This makes education in particular – or, more precisely, the denial of education – in a downright perverse way into the legitimation for excluding people from society. A socially just educational policy would have to expand education where social security is being phased out. For investing in education is the social insurance that comes after social insurance, as it were. It is also true that tuition fees and equality of opportunity are by no means mutually exclusive, though only when, first, the tuition fees are really used for the benefit of the universities alone and, second, are used to finance a model of loans and grants that reaches beyond national borders.

Another error of the current neoliberal agenda is to confuse the call for autonomy of the universities with market autonomy. This squanders a possibility which Humboldt already envisaged at the beginning of the nineteenth century, namely, organizing education and research at a remove from both the state and the market. The key lies in the self-financing of the universities, and this could be based in turn on a variety of funding sources: endowment capital, regional and global networks, tuition fees and, especially, patents. Thus universities could tap into sources of funding (as, for example, at the Massachusetts Institute of Technology in the United States) – also in order to protect the autonomy of the universities from the clutches of the economy.

Humboldt I pursued a national educational goal. The university became the birthplace of national sovereignty and of the national society. Humboldt II, by contrast, is founded on an educational policy 'Declaration of Interdependence'. Its core statement is that no nation can solve its problems on its own. Global problems create transnational commonalities. Interdependence is not a scourge of humankind but the precondition of its survival. The social and political lexicon must be rewritten accordingly. The Humboldt II university points us towards a humanity of reciprocal inter-dependence for which the struggle over the dignity of the excluded other acquires the status that class struggle had in the nineteenth century.

The global elites are jealously defending their new, transnational options. But what are they struggling for? For a pure economism? Or for a new constitution of freedom? That also differentiates Humboldt II from Humboldt I: the school of the nation is replaced by the school of world citizenship. Then it is once again a matter of educational substance, of curiosity and the thirst for learning, and not of the purely utilitarian fixation on lists of skills and didactic subtleties.

For the global domestic political agenda dares to turn the university into the laboratory of a second, post-national enlightenment. Since the latter exists only in rudimentary form, the unity of research and teaching remains indispensable. However, Humboldt II must distinguish between forms of the both/and which are more oriented to teaching and ones more oriented to research.

Humboldt I served to inculcate the national outlook, hence to train the national elites, and presupposed a corresponding educated middle-class milieu of civil servants and pay scales. Humboldt II serves to inculcate the cosmopolitan outlook. It trains the elites who are supposed to contribute to shaping the world society which is taking shape in struggles and wars at both the national and the international level. A both/and university is emerging, one which is both for national-cosmopolitan elites and for mass education. This simultaneity would have an important function: it could counteract the new global class cleavage which is already becoming established today – the cleavage between transnationally networked elites and territorially bound middle-class workers who see themselves as 'losers of globalization' and are barricading themselves behind their national worldview.

The local globality of Humboldt II is expressed in funding sources, research topics, forms of cooperation, curricula and globally recognized diplomas; but it also finds expression in the transnational background experiences of the research teams and in the policy of recruiting foreign students with different perspectives on the world. Humboldt II would have to become once again a place which makes the adventure of 'exploratory thought' possible, not least also as an answer to the world of global threats, of climate change, global economic crises, terrorism, AIDS. What better definition could there be of usefulness in a self-endangering civilization?

9

A Kind of Berlin Wall Has Again Collapsed

March 2010

The Swiss tax wall has collapsed, the state-sanctioned banking secrecy that represents a cornerstone of the national, global economic power system. What ultimately brought about its collapse is probably the freedom of information in the era of the Internet which it is difficult to restrict. What seemed to be built for eternity – the possibility of diverting black money into niche states which use the means provided by national sovereignty to transform the illegality of tax evasion into lucrative legality – dissolved into thin air overnight.

A conflict has been raging for weeks between Germany and Switzerland over the purchase of 'stolen' Swiss bank data by the German federal or state governments. Chancellor Angela Merkel and her finance minister Wolfgang Schäuble had decided to purchase the file containing information about German tax fugitives. Since then over 3,300 tax offenders have decided to make a voluntary declaration.

Moreover, the parasitic legal situation created and stabilized by national legal frontiers was replaced by a piece of global domestic politics. Switzerland is abandoning its self-delusion and is surrendering an element of (il)legal sovereignty. Now it wants to implement Article 26 of the OECD agreement as quickly as possible. This stipulates that the signatories should provide official assistance not only in cases of serious tax fraud but also in cases of suspected tax evasion. With this step, the Swiss are transforming what has until now been an essential element of national policy into global domestic policy. There are bringing their legislation into conformity with European and American standards.

As a result the Swiss will close their borders to black money from abroad. Untaxed money should no longer enter the country, according to Finance Minister Hans-Rudolf Merz. Moreover, foreigners who have deposited their black money there have to reckon with attempts by the Swiss to 'legalize' their assets. Here the perspective of national legal sovereignty no longer provides the standard of legality but the perspective of the foreign state affected by tax evasion. The language is also changing. Suddenly it is no longer a matter of civil rights but of 'tax dodgers' and 'offenders' who are now also supposed to pay a flat rate withholding tax of 25 per cent of capital gains on their deposits in the former tax haven Switzerland. Whether such a far-reaching amnesty for the tax dodgers can be negotiated in consultation with their countries of origin remains open.

Is an 'International of the nation states' in the offing?

But why call what has collapsed here a kind of 'Berlin Wall'? Isn't this formulation an exaggeration? No, this ending of banking secrecy has been discussed in legal and moral terms until now but not in terms of power strategy. Upholding banking secrecy not only serves to minimize taxes, to promote money-laundering, etc.

Besides it also offers global economic actors a considerable strategic power advantage. It enables them to utilize the difference between 'tax oases' and 'tax deserts' (that is, states which raise taxes – note the verbal imagery) in such a way that the latter are played off against the former.

To be sure, a politics that facilitates and conceals tax and capital flight has always had to expect to be branded as parasitic by global public opinion. Yet all attempts at global domestic political coordination and regulation seemed to be condemned to perpetual failure because those who refused to cooperate seemed to have a strategic power advantage on their side in the form of the protection of national sovereignty: they could spare themselves the effort of difficult negotiations and at the same time benefit from them as free riders by shielding their financial business from regulatory interference. Now this can no longer be taken for granted (to put it mildly). Is the shock of the financial crisis and of the state boycott giving rise to an 'International of the nation states' after all?

Yet global domestic politics can also mean that the national domestic politics of major global powers determines the law of action throughout the world. If climate policy is downplayed in the United States, then the necessary policy on climate within global domestic politics is blocked – or so it seems. What seemed obvious just a short time ago is suddenly up for grabs again. In November 2009, the world substantially agreed that CO_2 emissions are leading to global warming and that something must be urgently done about this, even though no consensus exists on what exactly should happen. On 7 December, fifty-six well-known newspapers throughout the world stated in a joint communiqué: 'The politicians in Copenhagen have the power to shape history's judgment on this generation: one that saw a challenge and rose to it, or one so stupid that we saw calamity coming but did nothing to avert it.'

The consensus on climate is collapsing

That almost sounds like a speech from times past, now that climate science is on trial and climate policy has lost its way. The climate debate in the United States, and hence in the world, seems to have become bogged down in a morass of political indecisiveness and familiar antagonisms. Unless appearances are deceptive, it will not be possible to fulfil the in any case vague promise of Copenhagen to limit the average global increase in temperature to 2°C, at any rate as far as the pivotal role of the United States is concerned. If the US administration is not able to prevail in Congress and in the Senate, then it will not be able to sign a new treaty. Without the United States, neither China nor India will give legally binding assurances. If the largest polluters in the world are not on board, then all efforts to restrict emissions will fail. The Obama administration has not given up just yet. But the failure of Kyoto seems to be repeating itself in a new form.

We need to remind ourselves of what many people have forgotten, namely, that Kyoto was essentially a US invention by means of which the Clinton administration was able to finance a climate policy without running aground on the domestic political rocks of a tax increase. The other countries signed the body of rules in the expectation that in this way they could win the commitment of the United States – then already not only the foremost military power but also the chief polluter – to the efforts to bring the warming of the atmosphere under control. Yet, although Clinton signed the treaty, Congress rejected the corresponding body of laws. Now something similar seems to be repeating itself following Copenhagen. The United States is trying to undo the laboriously assembled bouquet of prospective minimum norms while simultaneously making Europe responsible for the inefficiency of the cosmopolitical climate policy on account of its indecisiveness and contentiousness.

Interestingly, there are also disagreements on the US side in this regard. A coalition of sixteen US federal states and five Canadian provinces are working on implementing their own system aligned with the European model by 2012. But now this initiative is meeting with internal opposition in view of the doubts concerning the trustworthiness of the climate prognoses. In one of the member states of this coalition, Utah, politicians have passed a resolution stating that climate science is a 'conspiracy'. Arizona in turn abandoned the initiative with the excuse that the recession does not permit an effective climate policy. And California's impressive climate programme is coming under massive public pressure at a time when its most important proponent, Governor Arnold Schwarzenegger, is due to leave office this year.

Here it is becoming clear that global domestic politics itself gives rise to the resistance which threatens to thwart it. As long as it is assumed that the agreement of all polluters, or at least of the largest and most powerful polluters, is needed in order to make progress, the decisive veto power is being dropped into the lap of the chief polluters. This could be described pessimistically as the law of the self-obstruction of cosmopolitan climate policy. Climate change is giving rise to the very equality and commonality which can lend the antagonisms visibility and relevance for global domestic politics and allow them to run riot.

A post-Copenhagen model: regional climate policy from below

There are reports from global domestic politics, however, that delivers a contradictory message. Finland recently held an ambitious 'action summit' to rescue the Baltic Sea, which is suffering under decades-long environmental neglect and destruction. Political leaders from all of the nine Baltic littoral states and representatives of other affected countries, such as Norway, took part, as did representatives of the EU and approximately 1,500 delegates sent by regional organizations, companies, NGOs and local civil society groups. Angela Merkel did not see fit to attend the conference. By contrast, the Russian strong man, Vladimir Putin, attended and thereby demonstrated that a green heart is beating in Russia's breast.

In contrast to Copenhagen, which was organized on the top-down model, the focus of the organizers of this summit was on accentuating the initiative, ingenuity and competence of the participants in accordance with the opposite bottom-up model. At the same time, they fully welcomed the support of the governments. In Helsinki, in contrast to Copenhagen, over 140 specific undertakings and declarations on practical measures were adopted. Even multinational corporations, such as IBM and Nokia, though also local wood producers and farmers' associations, signed up. With justified pride, the organizers claimed to have created a post-Copenhagen paradigm.

What made the Helsinki summit a success? Ultimately probably its regionality – that is, on the one hand, the absence of the megapowers China and the United States, for that meant that the major inequality, the antithesis between the First and Third World, was absent; on the other, the Baltic risk community. In the meantime all of the Baltic littoral states and their populations are aware in a very specific sense of the dangers that the contamination of the Baltic poses for all of them.

This allows the assessment that under conditions of relative regional equality, environmental threats found a sense of commonality and community. A dynamic of conflict between winners and losers is emerging here too; but ultimately all participants could regard themselves as winners of an ecologized transnational politics.

The fact that Russia instrumentalized the summit for its own economic purposes speaks against this only in part. It is correct that this major power is expanding its proportion of the shipping traffic on the Baltic exponentially, as it is its oil, gas and other exports. But this very fact is creating the need to implement cross-border environmental standards. Climate policy is not a matter of compassion. If national security interests and economic self-interest combine to form a transnational political alliance under the banner 'Save the Baltic!' so much the better. For that contributes to a cosmopolitan realism which can lead (analogously to the emergence of national communities during the nineteenth century) to the emergence of cosmopolitan communities at the beginning of the twenty-first century.

What can be observed in Copenhagen and Helsinki are two contradictory constellations and manifestations of what I would like to call (in a somewhat old-fashioned spirit) the cosmopolitical dialectic of climate change and of environmental policy: the closer the world grows together as a result of climate change, the more it is divided by climate change.

The major question is of course: how do these contradictory processes fit together? Or, more precisely: under which conditions does collision win out and under which cooperation? Perhaps Copenhagen does in fact stand for the first case (radical global inequality) and Helsinki for the second (relative regional equality). This could finally mark the beginning of the work of a sociology of climate change which thematizes the issue of inequality and domination lurking in climate change and explains how the heightened awareness of the commonality of the danger can be used to create cosmopolitically open and interconnected national communities.

10

German Euro-Nationalism

April 2010

The first law of the world risk society is: never allow a global risk to go unused, because it is an opportunity to achieve something great, expand political cooperation and strengthen Europe!

When the euro was introduced, many opinionated economists warned that starting the monetary union before a political union had been established meant putting the cart before the horse. They were either unwilling or unable to understand that that was precisely the intention! The euro and the foreseeable follow-on problems were supposed to force the governments and countries trapped in national egoisms to achieve political and social coordination through the power of material self-interests.

Yet global domestic politics need not be multilateral and cosmopolitan but can also be associated with unilateral and national goals. Now we have a clear example of this: Chancellor Angela Merkel used the European monetary crisis to deflect the future course of financial policy in the euro zone in the direction of a German Europe. While the global financial risk made the world hold its breath, the governments were acclaimed because, to everyone's surprise, they took the political initiative in order to save the world economy from itself. Last year the banks were still the problem but now it is the governments themselves that are suddenly the problem. But who will rescue the states from a sovereign default?

The risk of a sovereign default is not synonymous with a sovereign default itself. Risk means the anticipation of a future catastrophe in the present. It must be distinguished from the actual, future future, which always remains unknown and uncertain. This distinction is important because assertions concerning risk conjure up the very future which is supposed to be prevented. Thus its logic conforms to the normativity of a self-refuting prediction. In this sense, the European governments are combating what until now was unthinkable, namely, the ghosts of possible sovereign defaults and the collapse of the euro, which are haunting the financial markets.

Just a short time ago, the euro was regarded as an anchor of stability in times of worldwide financial turbulence. Suddenly, the members of the European monetary union must confront the fundamental decision: cooperate or bust! I thought: 'My God, what an opportunity!' If the European Union did not exist, it would have to be invented to avert the collapse of the euro. Kant or catastrophe! A strong and stable euro presupposes the political will to take the policy of peace by other means (coordination and integration of economic policy) in the euro zone a decisive step further.

Or has the time come to defend Germany against Europe – to defend the successful German model of 'national, democratic, social market economy' against the attacks of its jealous European neighbours who want to remedy their budget deficits by grabbing into the German purse? Isn't a form of reciprocal nationalism the solution, as the pragmatic, national Europeans seem to think? On this view, each state has the autonomy and the duty to settle its own financial problems. At the same time, every nation must recognize the sovereignty of the other European nations, so that all of them avoid negative consequences of their economic policies for others. This view rests on three principles: equal rights, coordinated packages of measures and mutual responsibility. To these must be added a fourth principle: the competence of the EU in economic policy must not be extended. This model of reciprocal nationalism may work well under fair weather conditions. But it is destined to fail at a time when the euro is threatened with collapse. Incompatible budgetary and fiscal policies and incompatible social and taxation systems are becoming ticking political time bombs in the national and international domains. No country is strong enough to pull the others out of the quagmire. At the same time, it is becoming all too clear how closely they are all now interwoven: if one state goes bankrupt it threatens to drag others down with it into the abyss.

Currently perceived financial risks necessitate cooperation even when key actors such as the German chancellor see no reason for it – a further example of the cosmopolitical imperative: 'Cooperate or bust!' The reception for Chancellor Merkel was solemn but not hostile according to the reports after the EU summit in Brussels last week. By then she had already got her way in a dispute in which she stood alone against all of the other heads of government.

In the days leading up to the EU summit in Brussels, the German government had repeated like a mantra that the issue of a possible Greek sovereign default was not even on the order of business; in addition, it stated that a special meeting of the euro countries seemed to make little sense because it was not clear what was supposed to be decided. Then everything turned out differently in Brussels. Greece played a major role, there was a meeting and the euro states made a decision. The German side was at pains to point out that this meeting was not a formal working session but an 'aperitif' before the joint evening meal of the heads of state and government. The sixteen representatives of the euro states took their aperitif separately from the representatives of the countries which have not adopted the ailing single currency. Such are the ironical ways – in the guise of 'aperitif diplomacy' – in which the cosmopolitical imperative can exact compliance.

The risk crisis of the euro has led to the crystallization of new power relations. When the time comes to make decisions, neither the EU Commission nor the EU president nor the current holder of the rotating EU Council presidency acts. When the moment of truth comes the German chancellor acts in collaboration with French President Sarkozy. Angela Merkel is neither Angela Kohl nor Angela Brandt. After all, Chancellor Kohl stated in his government programme for the years 1991 to 1994: 'Germany is our fatherland, Europe our future.' And during the first session of the unified German Bundestag Willy Brandt stated: 'Germans and Europeans belong together now and, hopefully, for all time.' The turn given to this profession of faith by Merkel has touched a raw nerve not only among the European neighbours. Nor is the chancellor a Maggie Merkel who imposes the logic of the market in Europe with an iron hand. She is Angela Bush. Just as US President Bush Jr used the risk of terrorism to foist his unilateralism of war on the rest of the world, Angela Bush used the European financial risk to force German stability policy on the rest of Europe.

The Deutschmark was the currency of German power. The same is now supposed to hold for the euro. Deutschmark nationalism is being retrospectively and enduringly engraved on the euro now that it is threatened with collapse. In the name of 'Europe', the supreme premise of German post-war policy, multilateralism, was sacrificed to the need for 'euro stability' with a peculiar, Merkel-typical mixture of self-referentiality, hubris and self-deception.

There is nothing wrong with defending German interests. The core of the problem is the fact that these interests are misunderstood and are pursued on the model of a self-confirming prophecy as a national zero-sum game. As a result, the ghosts of nationalist politics are rising from their graves, as is shown for example by the atavistic smear campaign against Greece.

Merkel's attempt to contrive a German euronationalism fits into the larger picture. Whether the issue is the economy, foreign policy or overseas deployments of the Bundeswehr, the German chancellor speaks for a nation which is, as the French say, *'replié en soi'*, turned in on itself, a Germany which no longer embodies the European ambitions of Europeans but, on the contrary, plays down its European obligations and ties, a Germany which chooses a future as a 'greater Switzerland' and a 'little China' (export surpluses with low domestic demand), a Germany which redefines the meaning of German post-war constitutional history in the sense of a self-referential nation state ('the social market economy should come to the rescue of the globalized world') – hence, not least a Germany which stirs up Europe's 'German question' once again.

The post-war German model embodied high modern foreign policy: postnational, multilateral, economistic, highly peaceful in all areas, preaching interdependence in all directions, everywhere seeking friends, nowhere suspecting enemies; 'power' was almost a dirty word, to be replaced by 'responsibility'; national interests remained discreetly hidden, like a Biedermeier console, under a heavy tablecloth embroidered with the words 'Europe', 'Peace', 'Cooperation', 'Stability', 'Normality', even 'Humanity'. Is it really the case, or does it just seem, that the united Europe referred to in the preamble to the German constitution is no longer the guiding star either of German politics or of Germany's self-understanding? If this were so – and this question calls for a lively discussion within and outside Europe – then the best times for Germany and Europe would be past.

A very special Easter holiday

It also holds for the Catholic Church that the horror of child sexual abuse, which seems to be the product of the worst anti-papal fantasies, is an opportunity to achieve something great. God has sent the Church of the consecrated priestly sinners and the Pope the gift of the implacable attention of the mass media to lead them away from the path of moral self-destruction and onto the path of self-renewal. However, to date there are few signs that this gift of public confession will be accepted. Pope Benedict XVI's pastoral letter to the Irish Catholics caused annoyance not only in Ireland. The attempt to present the clerical abuse on the Emerald Isle, including the systematic cover-up, as a unique aberration patently contradicts the facts. Instead it serves the self-defence of the Vatican.

Since the sex abuse cases in Great Britain and Ireland from the early 1970s first became public, the attempts at appeasement both on the part of the officials and of devout Catholics themselves have changed direction several times. At first the ecclesiastical authorities declared that it was only a matter of a couple of bad apples; but the Ryan Report, which was submitted last summer, uncovered the decades-long systematic abuse of thousands of children in Ireland.

Another line of defence defined the problem as a specifically anglophone one whose roots lie in Ireland's expansive Catholic culture which was exported to the United States and Australia. Yet this explanation also collapsed after cases of abuse were uncovered throughout Europe (in Germany, the Netherlands, Austria, Switzerland, Italy, and elsewhere) and were denounced by the media. And then there is still the feeble excuse presented by the Pope that sexual abuse in the Church is connected with a wholescale breakdown of values in the secular era. That stands the causal relation on its head. After all, it is precisely the implementation of modern law, which includes basic rights for children and the freedom of the press that made public the sexual abuse of children, which may have been going on for a very long time and been knowingly tolerated by the Church hierarchy.

This is why now is the time for the major, long-overdue reform of the Catholic Church, a reform for which it may be able to draw the strength only from the implacable attention of the worldwide mass media. Abolish celibacy, the prohibition of women priests and the demonization of the pill; all three positions are the result of a neurotic fixation on sexuality. That would in fact be a special Easter holiday. Jesus also died for the errant church – and for the faith in its resurrection in this world.

11

Beyond the Aeroplane

Was the volcanic ash farce, coming after the commotion over the swine flu, merely a further example of how quickly we succumb to collective hysteria? Or was there more to it? Already in the 1960s Hannah Arendt raised the irritating question: what happens when the labouring society runs out of labour (because of advances in automation)? The Eyjafjallajökull ash cloud has made the world the gift of a magnificent 'critical experiment' and forced us with existential implacability to confront the question: what happens when all flights are cancelled in the air travel society (*in der Fluggesellschaft*)?* Volcano mimics natural trade union: if it be my strong ash's will, the global air traffic will stand still! (leaving the complicity of the wind aside for the moment).

Climate change raised the issue: is there a (mobile) life after the motorcar? Suddenly the next problem arises:

---

*Note that there is a play on words here which gets lost in translation: '*Fluggesellschaft*' is the German word for 'airline' but in the context of the present chapter is also used in the literal sense of 'flight-society', which is more intelligibly rendered as 'air travel society'. *Trans.*

what comes after the aeroplane? Was that perhaps a foretaste of the future, of the post-jet age? Whether it be work, the motorcar or the aeroplane – what once seemed to be contrary to human nature has become so much 'second nature' to us that we do not even dare to imagine a labouring society without jobs for everyone, a motorcar society without cars for everyone or an air travel society without flights for everyone. However, precisely this imagining what is inconceivable is becoming necessary.

The inestimable merit of the ash cloud critical experiment is that it made crystal-clear that, given the way we live and think and given the way modern society is organized, we are condemned to fly! Without aeroplanes we are like Beckettian stage figures, body fragments, living torsos, whose world and lives are out of joint. We all want to or have to fly out and back as quickly as possible to do business or give the appearance of doing business, to nod off at conferences or endure family gatherings, to catch a breath of package holiday air or conduct a long-distance love affair.

As I write these lines I am sitting in the slow train between Trondheim and Östersund that is serving as a substitute for the aeroplane – which in no way mitigates the beauty of the fjord glistening in the evening light. Why is that remarkable? Because it exhibits a characteristic feature of global domestic politics. What has actually occurred? Nothing. And that nothing has occurred is the point.

It was not a disaster (such as the crash of the Polish government jet which led to the death of President Lech Kaczynski and his entourage) that triggered the total ban on flying in Europe but the anticipation of such a catastrophe. And this envisaging the disaster in order to prevent it rested on nothing more or less than computer simulation models. The fact that nothing occurred, that no plane crashed, is taken by some to be proof of the correctness of the measures taken, by others to be proof of the hysteria and wrongness of the measures taken.

But it must be asked: must the catastrophe which is supposed to be prevented first occur in order to ensure that the measures taken to prevent it are recognized and known to be appropriate? Then the measures taken would always be wrong, either because a disaster didn't occur or because one did occur.

However, the not easily calculable risk alone that something bad could happen is suddenly ever-present and is creating a new commonality of situations across all borders, namely, the choice between waiting game and odyssey. For I am sharing my adventure with many millions of stranded passengers who are now prevented from taking off and are either trying to reach their destination on the ground (e.g. with transcontinental taxi rides) or have to sleep on camp beds with kit and caboodle in eerily deserted airport halls.

Our 'we' is a colourful mixture including the most diverse income groups, every conceivable skin colour and nationality, people with and without visas, Christians and Muslims, agnostics and esoterics. But all of us share a momentary characteristic that fundamentally defines our situation here and now. We form the diaspora community of fate, fragmented into countless thousands of individual destinies strewn across the globe, of the 'living side effects' of the staged threat, not of the volcano cloud which rehearses the rebellion of nature against civilization.

Volcano clouds have always existed and in and of themselves they do not pose a threat. They only become a threat within the horizon of the globalized and constantly expanding air travel industry. The 'side effects fate' into which our mobile form of life shattered for a historical moment reflects how the globalized air traffic system is at the mercy of 'internalized nature'. The volcanic ash cloud is the cow on the motorway, an 'enemy' of the airlines and the 'air travel society'. Pilots treat this stunningly beautiful cloud, whose images enchanted the evening news, with great respect by avoiding any contact with it and giving it a wide berth. When volcanoes spew ash and smoke, airlines with experience of volcanoes like Alaska Airlines assemble their fleet on the ground and put protective plastic coverings over their parked aeroplanes. 'We have been flying now for over a century but the volcanoes have existed a lot longer and, to be honest, they are winning', said a flight captain.

Like a cabaret act, the same spectacle is being presented over and over again with changing actors. Those who are supposed to regulate, the politicians and experts, waver between ignorance and hysteria. Either they brush the risks under the carpet or they dramatize them – and often they do both at different times for different audiences.

Do you recall the back and forth over the swine flu? In the end, millions of vials of vaccine remained in storage. Or the Chernobyl cloud, the radioactive cloud which struck terror into Europe after the 'communist' (Franz Josef Strauss) reactor disaster twenty-four years ago? Atomic energy, so it was claimed at the time and is again being claimed today, is absolutely safe. Or '9/11'? Shortly before the terrorist attack those who warned that such an attack was possible were ridiculed and declared to be crazy. Afterwards hysteria over terrorism was stoked in order to justify foreign invasions.

And now the ongoing global drama of the financial crisis! First the stage direction was: Keep quiet! Down with the critical voices who point out the organized irresponsibility of the business with risk. Then the monstrosity was spelt out and the economically and morally bankrupt large banks were spoonfed back to health with billions of public money. In the meantime, the entire blame is being laid at the door of Greece, even though everyone knows that the risk of sovereign default is haunting Spain, Italy, perhaps most of all Great Britain and at least also some municipalities in wealthy Germany. The euro is going up in flames!

For a few days the world was turned on its head. Ministers of transport, whose very existence had been a well-guarded secret, suddenly became the lords of the skies. Compensation claims rained down in torrents; legal systems were unable to process the cases. And everywhere the same mantra: 'The volcanic cloud came out of the clear blue sky – nobody could foresee it.' And: 'Safety is our first priority!'

Which safety? For, after all, the risk of a crash gives rise to the risk of a bankruptcy in the blink of an eye. A conflict breaks out between the disasters which are threatening which plunges the decision-makers into a dilemma: should I uphold the ban on flying with the result that the ('system-relevant') airline industry slides into bankruptcy and the virtually bankrupt states must also rescue them? Or should I give the all-clear for flights to resume and then a plane crashes nonetheless – and with it my popularity ratings?

We crave certainty. We are not willing to accept that, as the magnitude of the impending disaster increases, the assertion that the probability of its occurring is low becomes meaningless. The result is that it is becoming increasingly difficult to make a clear and binding distinction between hysteria and deliberate fear-mongering, on the one hand, and appropriate fear and precaution, on the other.

The innocent beauty of the Icelandic volcanic cloud even encapsulates the current state of Europe. The European countries have only agreed to administer the upper airspace jointly through an air traffic control centre. It only deals with aeroplanes that want to overfly the continent at a great elevation. But anyone who wants to land or take off, and thus to feel European ground under their feet, enters the nation state jungle. Under the direction of Lufthansa, Germany has transformed itself overnight into a new kind of 'air travel society at your own risk', as it were. The airlines can request permission for 'visual flights' for which the air traffic control declines any responsibility. In such cases, the jets also fly through layers of the atmosphere with residues of volcanic ash without even a modicum of greater clarity having been gained about the real problem: is the cloud dangerous or not? This raises in turn the further question of whether it would not be possible to lay down threshold values for the hazardousness of the volcanic ash. In theory, yes, in practice, no, for this contradicts not only the conflictuality of the interests but also above all the boundless lack of coordination of the regulatory authorities.

This makes it clear that global domestic politics is also what happens and remains when our most mundane problems become global but the institutionalized 'answers' remain national. Airspace is sovereign space and if the nations were to cede control over it then – and this is the crux of the matter – they would not only lose, but would first acquire, sovereignty in an age in which one thing can be said with certainty: the global air traffic business can no longer be regulated at the national level (any more than can the global business with financial transactions). Then the passengers would be spared the critical experiment of the chaos that played out with the completely arbitrary opening and closure of airports and air spaces throughout Europe. Thus the ash cloud recapitulated the political didactic play presented over and again by the financial crisis and by the terrorist attack of September 11, mad cow disease and many other examples: it could be so much easier if people, interest groups and politicians abandoned the antiquated notion of national sovereignty and recognized that sovereignty can be recovered only through global domestic politics based on cooperation, consultation and negotiation.

My trip to Scandinavia is now almost over and I am typing the last lines on the ferry from Gothenburg to Kiel. Now the calm insignificance of the sea stretching off into the darkness is surprising (or should I say 'calming', 'reassuring'?). The moon is shining, having no other choice, on the grey emptiness of the familiar sight that now seems surprisingly new.

Aeroplanes are heedless of space. They have no notion of the attractions of places. They only know non-places, the never-changing nowhere of airports. Who would want to deny that flying emancipates? Yet isn't flying also a soulless form of maximally rapid movement which is ignorant and destructive of the meaning of deceleration and the astonishment of earthbound travel? What I first suffer, but then experience, is the abrupt transition from air miles gluttony to a travel diet. Please, no false romanticism that glorifies travel in the age of horse-drawn coaches! The very notion that in a world without aeroplanes donkeys could carry us over the Alps is not exactly liberating.

12

Global Domestic Politics from Below: How Global Families Are Becoming Normal

June 2010

A couple from Germany waited over two years for their twins born of an Indian surrogate mother. The German authorities did not issue the children born in India a passport because surrogate motherhood is prohibited by German law. The authorities in India, where surrogate motherhood is legal, regarded the children as German citizens because their parents are German. As a result they refused to issue the twins Indian travel documents.

Therefore the father, an art historian, fought doggedly before German and Indian courts to be able to bring his 'stateless children' to Germany. With success: the Indian authorities finally broke down and issued passports and these have now been supplied with visas for entry into Germany. The parents can now adopt their 'own' children in Germany through an international legal procedure – 'as an exception' and on 'humanitarian grounds' (Federal Foreign Office).

Every fourth child currently born in Germany has a mother or a father with a foreign passport. Every third child under the age of five has an immigrant background, that is, either the child or at least one of its parents was born abroad and/or has a foreign passport. Even in cities like Stuttgart or Darmstadt people from over 140 nations are living alongside each other. The more colourful the national origin, the greater the linguistic and religious diversity within a population (hence within families, schools, medical practices, parliaments, etc.), the lower the contraction and ageing of a society. In the West the paradoxical fact is that nations that want to survive have to internalize the world.

These few socio-structural empirical indicators already reflect the dramas of the internal self-globalization of families which are being played out on the stages of everyday life throughout the world. Thus there is not only a macro-global domestic politics from above but also a micro-global domestic politics from below – in many places and in diverse forms. Let us consider a couple of examples.

Advocacy movements: Politics not only takes place in the institutions signposted for this purpose (parliaments, governments, etc.) but also in the simultaneously local and global ('glocal') civil society networks and initiatives; these represent the antipodes of mobile capital and of states. They often form rainbow coalitions and operate as advocates, creators and judges of cosmopolitan values and norms by inflaming and staging global public outrage over flagrant violations of norms with reference to concrete individual cases (environmental scandals, biographies of torture victims, etc.).

Schools, which are geared to national consensus and integration, are becoming 'small-scale global schools' inadvertently and generally without acknowledging it. Any schoolteacher who has to cope with multiethnic children speaking fifteen or more different native languages knows the meaning of global domestic politics from below: classrooms become places in which misunderstandings and antagonisms break out, but also places in which a wealth of national heritages unfolds which must nevertheless be reconciled and tolerated.

Medical practices and clinics: These are also meeting places of nations and religions; correspondingly, this internal globalization of the healthcare system leads to clashes between the notions of life and death, health and illness, associated with religious or secular worldviews. This clash of cultures also causes the premises of 'rational', 'white', 'Western', 'capitalist' medicine to totter.

Art and artists have also long since broken out of the national, self-enclosed mental ruts and ways of thinking. The 'global domestic political art' invented by Aby Warburg with his picture atlas is a kind of 'Dada knowledge machine' that makes it possible to amalgamate disparate and antithetical horizons of experience and symbolic worlds or set them on a collision course.

Finally, the *monotheistic religions* are by their very origins global players; religion is in this sense the ultimate border crossing – 'God needs no passport' (Peggy Levitt).

The fact that the family has long since become the crime scene of a global domestic politics from below is shown by our opening example. As a result of advances in reproductive medicine, birth and parenthood can be uncoupled and (like jobs) be actively 'outsourced' by exploiting legal contradictions between countries. The room for action opened up by medical technology makes it possible to organize conception, pregnancy and parenthood across national borders. What used to be called simply giving birth to a child is now being split up into the 'egg donor mother', the 'birth mother' and the 'social mother'. Connecting these different types of mothers socially inevitably becomes an obstacle race between the antitheses dividing the national legal systems.

Yet that is just one case among many. One could cite, in addition, immigrant families, transnational motherhood, bi-national and bi-religious families, transnational children, 'parachute children' (as children are called who are chosen by their families of origin to acquire degrees in distant countries and establish 'family base camps' there, as it were), arranged marriages, long-distance love, commuter relationships and, last but not least, transnational grandparents.

As Elisabeth Beck-Gernsheim shows in her studies on transnational families, people struggle to achieve an image of community which does not rest on homogeneity and consensus but on known and recognized diversity: 'it is not the resemblances, but the differences which resemble each other' (Lévi-Strauss). That is neither the demise of the nation (as many people fear) nor the transition to cosmopolitan global solidarity (as many hope). However, the statement 'The global other is living in our midst' here acquires a concrete, familial meaning.

In an attempt to understand the logics of action and contradictions with which people have to cope who live across, through and against borders, I propose to distinguish between philosophical cosmopolitanism, whose spiritual home is cloud cuckoo land, and a 'really existing cosmopolitanism'. The latter is not, as is suggested by the parallel formula of 'really existing socialism', for example, a social and political project which has gone off the historical rails. On the contrary, here an unrecognized and unconceptualized reality is emerging (often unintentionally and invisibly) which is of major relevance for everyday life, involves explosive potentials and ambivalences and cuts across the categories of nation, territory and state which have become second nature. It is a volcanic reality, one which it is easy to overlook, however, if our outlook is nationally programmed or is guided by speculative cosmopolitanism. The attempts just to acknowledge, not to mention understand, this 'social thing' (Durkheim) of a cosmopolitan political realism (in families, social movements, religions, etc.) are in their infancy.

Global domestic politics from below inevitably collides with the world of national institutions; it operates in a space which can be called 'translegal'. Someone who lives and operates across borders must utilize the gaps and antitheses which exist and emerge between legal systems. Thus he or she acts 'translegally' in the sense that, measured by national legal standards, he or she is generally not yet acting illegally but, measured by the standards of the national community of solidarity, he or she is often no longer acting legitimately.

We think in terms of antitheses between 'Western' and 'non-Western', 'European' and 'non-European' countries, in order to find our bearings in the landscapes of the modern world. However, these 'separate worlds' often coexist within a single family. The notion that Western secularism/atheism and Muslim religions, Christianity and Buddhism, belong to different parts of the world, also fails to understand the hybrid forms within families. Thus, in so-called 'Muslim families' in Europe or the United States, a daughter may inhabit the world of Western atheism, whereas her sister and one of her brothers inhabit the world of Muslim fundamentalism and her father insists on the eternal prerogatives of the male supposedly written down in the Koran. How can a single family endure what divides the world?

The family reality which is lived out here contradicts the organic metaphors in terms of which we think of the 'family': husband and wife often cannot live 'side by side'; conflicts cannot be resolved 'face to face'; one shows solidarity not only by standing 'shoulder to shoulder', walking 'arm in arm'. Family is not only realized in 'face-to-face' relations.

The green card holder is the elect!

Key concepts such as 'emigration' or 'immigration' already suggest a false finality, a false either-here-or-there.

Migration often means planned family advancement across continents. The foundation is a kind of mutually beneficial contractual arrangement. The decision to emigrate is a family decision and it is based on the calculation of maximizing the expected utility and minimizing the risks for the entire family.

In order to make this collective family advancement across the closely guarded borders of the world society a reality, individuals are tested and selected, even trained. They should be clever, mature, self-confident and talented and know how to communicate with the 'whites' in order to make their fortune in Europe or the United States. The 'unification of the family' across borders is the explicit aim of all preparations and the key criterion for the 'success' of the advancement of the family. The migrant who arrives in the promised land like an 'anchor child' only appears to act as an isolated individual; in fact he is operating within a relational network of obligations. After all, families have even sold part of their possessions to support one of their members.

How the disparity between unequal worlds impacts on the most intimate domain – marriage – was expressed bluntly in a marriage advertisement from India. According to the description, the woman who was looking for a husband was from a good family, light-skinned and a member of the Brahmin caste; in short, she possessed the status characteristics which are highly valued in Indian society. The ideal future husband, by contrast, could be described in a few words: he should be a green card holder! From the perspective of countries undergoing development, this possession promises the inestimable value of advancement through migration – not just for the daughter, but for the entire family.

Someone who is at a disadvantage on the marriage market of the destination country on account of his income and status is at an advantage on the marriage market of his country of origin. Be it a green card or verified residence status in Germany: someone who can produce such a document is at the very top of the hierarchy in the country of origin. This increases the marriage prospects of migrants enormously – and, conversely, it increases their readiness to choose a wife from the old country. In this sense, it is no surprise that the economic gulf between First and Third Worlds delves deep into the private life of transpacific Vietnamese couples, for example. The decisive insight, however, is that the alliance they forge is not simply a continuation of the ethnic-religious traditions which they have brought with them from the home country and unpacked on arrival in the host country. Instead it is shaped by disparities with regard to advancement and decline between the separate worlds which are supposed to be connected in the marriage. And it is shaped likewise by the experience of immigration, of the new arrival in a strange country and by the status and the practical opportunities to which this gives rise for those left at home, on the one hand, and for those who have left for the new world, on the other. The central point is the twofold horizon, the relation of tension between the 'there' world and the 'here' world, which gives rise to completely new motivations.

Misunderstanding as liberation

For many people, a home, a passport and an identity are the secular version of the Holy Trinity constituting the family. Yet families have long since split apart and practise a kind of solidarity between strangers, at times reaching across continents. Here too struggles take place over the values of freedom, equality and democracy – but, in a clash of cultures which must be conducted and endured in the internal space of intimacy.

It is a historical error, therefore, simply to assume that families are 'essentially' territorial families, just as the assumption that states are 'essentially' territorial states is incorrect. On the contrary, there are transnational families, just as there are transnational corporations and transnational states (e.g., in rudimentary form, the EU). This raises the question: can transnational families offer cross-border networks of reciprocity, mutual responsibility and justice as a counterweight to turbocapitalism? Is there a future for the family as lived global domestic politics?

'Why are we actually conducting this bicultural marriage?', asks an American woman who lives with her Swiss husband across continents. 'The telephone bills are exorbitant, the travel expenses as well, we never fully understand each other and part of our collective self is always missing.' He answers: 'Because horizons have opened up for me that would otherwise have remained closed. Without our misunderstanding I would feel like a prisoner of my own culture.'

13

The Environmental Storm
on the Bastille

July 2010

Why hasn't the oil spill following the sinking of the Deepwater Horizon drilling platform, one of the worst environmental disasters in US history, led to the environmental storm on the Bastille of Big Oil? Why aren't the most urgent problems of our time – environmental crises and climate change – being met with the same energy, idealism and forward-looking democratic spirit as past tragedies of poverty, tyranny and war? Or will the loss of the Deepwater Horizon perhaps one day be referred to as the environmental Red October of Big Oil capitalism? The current state of the oil industry is reminiscent of the *Ancien Régime* on the eve of the Revolution.

The oil disaster in the Gulf of Mexico is bringing many truths to light. First, there is the incompetence and indifference demonstrated by the oil company BP. But there is also the failure of the public controllers. What was hitherto commended as an economic stimulus policy is now suddenly regarded as reprehensible 'collusion with scoundrels'. In view of the horrifying images of oil gushing into the ocean, environmental versions of ancient dramas are being played out on all cultural stages. Among the spectacles are dragons and dragon slayers, odysseys, deities and demons, only now they respond to technical formulas and assume the guise of BP boss Tony Hayward and US President Barack Obama.

The BP boss is donning sackcloth and ashes and speaking of an 'unprecedented series of mishaps'. At a hearing in the US House of Representatives, a Democratic congressman confronted him with the long list of BP disasters and in so doing brought another truth to light: there are still hundreds, even thousands of oil platforms belonging to BP, Exxon, Shell and other major oil companies operating in this region alone, but also throughout the world.

'Until the last hundredweight of fossil fuel is burnt up . . .'

To single BP out for blame is shabby. Deepwater Horizon is the symbol for the creeping demise of a global experiment, a model of growth based on exploiting fossil resources which is now shaking human self-confidence in view of environmental crises and climate change. And the important point is that no one can claim they didn't see it coming.

For the past two centuries, engines and machines have been driven by combustion and steam. Their discovery laid the foundation for economic prosperity to the present day. In the meantime, however, a whole generation has grown up in the knowledge that, given the limited nature of oil resources, the global victory march of a fossil fuel-based, and especially an oil-based, industry is burning up its own foundations. Already more than century ago, Max Weber anticipated the end of oil-based capitalism when he spoke of a time when 'the last hundredweight of fossil fuel is burnt up'. In the meantime this fossil-fuelled economy is working valiantly on its own demise as though there were no alternative. However, that makes a mockery of common sense. Why should a world which every day receives several times its energy needs from the sun, a free and inexhaustible energy source, look on impassively as clouds of oil spewing out of a hole 1,500 metres beneath the ocean surface choke all life to death?

Here the much-vaunted innovative power of capital and the utopian enthusiasm of engineers are in fact needed. 'Swords into ploughshares' was the motto of the peace movement. The motto of the environmental movement is: 'Deserts into energy sources!'

As the oil gushes forth, the truth is seeping out in dribs and drabs. 'We underestimated the complications involved in drilling for oil at a depth of 1,500 metres', confesses the penitent sinner Hayward. No one has the necessary safety technology to prevent or respond to such a worst-case scenario. It is not the failures but the victories that render the risks taken in the process uncontrollable. The engineers have become increasingly daring in their search for oil, they have bored at ever greater depths on the assumption that the potentially fatal side effects of their successes were controllable (just as the financial wizards and mathematical economists assumed that the risks of toxic loans were controllable). The depressing realization is that the 'residual risk' of deep drilling rests on non-knowing.

Should the safety technology employed fail, BP estimates that it would take two to four years for the oil to discharge completely from the well into the sea. Imagine that: 60,000 barrels of oil – day after day! But that is not all. We would be confronted for years (at least as long as the interest of the media held up) with a flood of images of polluted beaches and oil-soaked birds. That would signal the end of Big Oil capitalism – and of the policies which sustain this zombie industry.

'BP' = Beyond Petroleum

Faced with this ongoing disaster which threatens the security of the American people, not to mention its political survival, President Obama has declared 'war' on the black enemy from the deep. Now he, too, has his war in the Gulf – of Mexico. In fact, the oil disaster presents the world's greatest military and economic power as a kind of failed state. And Obama is in danger of becoming a 'failed president'. This reflects the failure of military thinking in the world risk society in which the greatest dangers for humanity no longer come from outside, from enemy states, but from within, from the so-called 'unseen and unintended side effects' of economic, scientific and political action. Trustees are becoming suspects and perpetrators. They no longer count as managers of risk, but as sources of risk.

What is the 'dragon slayer', the 'commander-in-chief', supposed to do? Send out his submarine fleet to torpedo the oil leak? Deploy troops against the management of BP 'and its sponsors'? In his 'war on terror', George W. Bush ordered an attack on the alleged countries of origin (Afghanistan and Iraq). In Obama's 'war on the gushing oil', should Great Britain by analogy be held responsible as the country of origin of the 'attack' on the American coast and the US population? In fact, President Obama unfailingly stresses the adjective 'British' when speaking of the energy company, as though British troops were again besieging Washington in order to burn down the White House as they did in 1814.

The traditional brand British Petroleum has long since been overtaken by its globalization destiny. Just as nowadays the trademark 'Made in Germany' is emblazoned even on products which were not made in Germany, British Petroleum has long ceased to be British. For the company merged with the US oil giant

Amoco in 1998 and took the opportunity, in a spirit of anticipatory environmental conformism, to banish the adjective 'British' and replace it with the optimistic green word 'beyond', so that the abbreviation BP now stands for 'Beyond Petroleum'. Could it be that wise foresight of the calamity played godfather at this re-baptism? Does the post-oil era begin with BP?

Here, at the latest, it becomes apparent that global domestic politics also makes possible a new variety of organized irresponsibility. Anyone who believes they have caught 'British' Petroleum (BP) *in flagrante* must learn the lesson that they are dealing with a company which also belongs to Americans, whose drilling rigs are built by Koreans and which pays its company tax to the Swiss inland revenue in Bern. (Thus 'BP' also stands for 'Bern Petroleum'!)

In the repositories of the still-to-be-founded museum of the world risk society the symbols of the unintentionally ironic once-in-a-century mistakes are already piling up. In the 1950s, the advice in the case of a nuclear explosion was: 'Duck and cover!' In order to protect yourself from nuclear contamination, you were supposed to take cover under the table or hold your briefcase over your head. Just as the Chernobyl nuclear disaster was dismissed as a failure of a 'communist' reactor, the blame for the demise of Deepwater Horizon is now being shifted onto the new friend-enemy as a 'British' disaster (in an ironic inversion of the British-American 'special relationship'). The commander-in-chief of the world's foremost military power needs, in his own words, 'an ass to kick'.

The safety technology of the engineers once again resembles the oft-cited bicycle brake on an intercontinental airliner. Under German administrative law, the Chernobyl reactor disaster did not exist because, in virtue of the definitional power of the law, only German nuclear power plants can cause German disasters.

American law provides for maximum compensation of seventeen million dollars in the case of oil disasters. Barack Obama imposed a fine of twenty billion dollars on the 'perpetrator' company responsible – to begin with. But under the thumbscrew pressure of global public opinion, BP now admits that the disaster will probably cost at least twice as much.

A policy which has now finally become a realistic option and seeks to overcome this 'once-in-a-century mistake' would also have to take into account changes in global relations of power. China, India, Brazil and African countries will not agree to any international approach which seeks to place limits on their efforts to achieve economic parity – and rightly so!

CO_2 emissions as the measure of all things

Is environmental policy nothing other than a global sale of indulgences for CO_2 sins? Or does environmental policy have the courage to project and realize a new age of solar energy in which prosperity no longer rests on environmental sins?

In the technocratic iron cage of environmental policy, CO_2 emissions are becoming the measure of all things. How much CO_2 is produced by using an electric toothbrush as opposed to a traditional one? 94.5g vs. 0g. How much does an electric alarm clock produce as opposed to a mechanical one? 22.26g vs. 0g. In the Christian vision of salvation, milk and honey flow in Paradise, but the consumption of milk on earth leads directly to environmental death. The 'climate killer' cow produces a couple of litres of methane gas per day, the equivalent of almost a kilogram of CO_2 per litre of milk.

Obama solemnly promised the nation and the world: 'The time has come . . . to fully embrace a clean energy future.' Thus, it could be time for the storm on the

'Bastille of Petroleum' to begin. The disaster in the Gulf of Mexico may be a watershed in the history of the United States. Obama could impose his stamp on the future if he were really to ring in the era 'Beyond Petroleum'.

14

Without Buddha I Could Not Be a Christian

August 2010

What differentiates Catholics from non-Catholics? This question sounds trivial, but in fact numerous studies show that it is highly contentious. In non-Catholic Christian contexts – for example, in the United States where Catholic identity was constructed through a demarcation from a largely Protestant society – the category was for a long time clearly identifiable. But that time is now past. A research group has established that today Catholics no longer see themselves as so different and they no longer have to demarcate themselves from others. They feel more liberated and empowered to make their own choices independently of whether they want to be loyal churchgoing Catholics, ethnic Catholics, private Catholics, merely *pro forma* Catholics or Catholics of Buddhist faith. The boundary between Catholic and non-Catholic is becoming blurred and the social environment no longer forces anyone to assume an identity either.

If one goes by the definition of 'Catholic' or 'non-Catholic' in the publications of the Vatican, it remains the case that only those people are Catholic who were baptized in accordance with the Catholic rite and have entrusted themselves to the leadership of the Catholic Church. Recent studies show, however, that the majority of American Catholics do not satisfy this decisive criterion. Fifty-eight per cent of the Catholics surveyed answered that one can very well be a good Catholic without adhering to the doctrinal prohibition on abortion; sixty-six per cent affirm that there is no incompatibility between being a good Catholic and being divorced and remarried; and seventy-five per cent state that one can very well be a good Catholic without following the teaching on birth control. Thus religion is becoming increasingly uncoupled from religiosity.

To speak of religion is already to fall prey to a Eurocentrist bias. For religion is conceived in substantive terms, whereby a clearly delimitable social repertoire of symbols and practices is assumed which prescribe an either/or. One can *either* believe the doctrine of the Resurrection or of the immaculate conception of Mary, and so on, *or* not; one cannot be a member of one religious community and simultaneously belong to another one. The adjective 'religious', by contrast, does not refer to membership of a particular organization or group. Instead it defines a stance on existential questions which concern the situation and self-understanding of human beings in the world. This not only invalidates the strict demarcation from the religious others (adherents of other faiths, atheists) but it also opens up the possibility of an internal pluralization of religions in the sense of multiple memberships or even of multiple conversions.

What is meant by this is expressed in the title of a book by the American theologian Paul Knitter: *Without Buddha I Could Not Be a Christian*. What makes this book so remarkable is that the perspective on the other is not laid down in one direction or another in accordance with the either/or schema. Instead the permanent change in perspective or, more specifically in this case, change in religion (the conversion to Buddhism and then the reconversion to the Christian tradition) leads to a deepening and enrichment of religious consciousness. In this way what seems to be 'religious promiscuity' within the horizon of the ecclesiastical monopoly on the truth could in fact ground the so urgently needed interreligious toleration. Cosmopolitans are in this sense multiple converts.

God is dangerous

Religion posits one feature as absolute, namely, the faith. Measured against this, all other social differences and antagonisms are inconsequential. The New Testament teaches us that all people are equal before God. This equality, this abolition of the boundaries separating human beings, groups, societies and cultures is the basis on which the (Christian) religions operate. However, the result is that, with the same absoluteness with which the distinctions between the social and political are abolished, a new fundamental distinction and hierarchy is established in the world, namely, that between believers and unbelievers. According to this distinction, the unbelievers (likewise in accordance with the dualistic logic) are threatened with damnation and in this sense are deprived of the status of human beings. Religions can build bridges between people where hierarchies and boundaries exist; at the same time, they open up new religious chasms between human beings where none previously existed.

The humanitarian universalism of the believers is founded on the identification with God – and on the demonization of the opponents of belief in God, who, as Saint Paul and Luther put it, are 'servants of Satan'. The seed of religiously motivated violence resides in the universalism of the equality among believers which deprives adherents of other faiths and unbelievers of what it promises the faithful, namely, fellow-human dignity and the community of equals in a world of strangers.

That is the worry which is becoming widespread, namely, that the reverse side of the failure of secularization is the threat of a new era of darkness. The ministers of health have issued a warning: religion can kill. Religion should not be peddled to youths under the age of eighteen.

An impressive illustration of the demonization of the religious other is the so-called 'mixed marriages war' which raged between the Catholic and Protestant Christians during the long nineteenth century and continues in the twenty-first century. This denominational fundamentalism, which refuses to see and recognize the 'unbeliever' as another Christian, is increasingly meeting with emphatic rejection, especially among active believers. Here, as Hans Joas reports, a reversal of the burden of proof has taken place as regards ecumenical cooperation: 'Increasingly justification is required when this does not take place, not when it takes place.'

This raises the question: does the Janus-faced character of brotherly love and enmity towards adherents of other faiths mainly apply to the official church doctrine but not to the practice of the believers and thus, to put it more pointedly, to 'religion' but not to 'religious'? Can the violence-laden, monotheistic either/or be relativized, subverted or defused by this syncretistic both/and toleration?

In Western societies which have internalized the principle of individual autonomy, individuals are increasingly autonomously inventing those minor religious narratives – the 'God of one's own' – which fit with one's 'own' life and one's 'own' horizon of experience. This 'God of one's own', however, is no longer the one God who dictates salvation by seizing control of history and authorizing intolerance and violence. Are we experiencing, under the banner of the 'God of one's own', a reversion of the monotheism of religion into a polytheism of religions?

That this syncretistic toleration is not only spreading secretly in the space of free-floating religiosity but is also practised as a matter of course in religious institutions can be shown by the example of Japan. There people see no problem in visiting a Shinto shrine at certain times of the year, celebrating a wedding according to the Christian rite and a Buddhist monk presiding over their burial. The sociologist of religion, Peter L. Berger, quotes the Japanese philosopher, Hajime Nakamura, who encapsulates this attitude: 'The West is responsible for two fundamental errors. The one is monotheism – there is only one God – and the other is the Aristotelian principle of contradiction: either A or not-A. Every intelligent person in Asia knows that there are many gods and that things can be both A as well as not-A.'

As the boundaries between Catholics and non-Catholics are becoming fluid, a new line of conflict is opening up which may be extremely important in the future, namely, the conflict between those currents of belief that allow room for doubt, that even see in it a moment of salvation of religion, and those which barricade themselves within the constructed 'purity' of their faith in order to repel doubt. 'Hard religions have a lot to offer consumers', according to the theologian Friedrich Wilhelm Graf; 'a strong, stable identity, a crisis-resistant interpretation of the world and history, orderly family structures and dense networks of solidarity.'

Combating the 'dictatorship of relativism', Pope Benedict XVI defends the Catholic hierarchy of truth which follows a skat logic: faith trumps reason; Christian faith trumps all other religions (in particular, Islam).

And the Pope is the supreme trump in the skat deck of truth of Catholic orthodoxy.

History teaches us that the deification of the nation leads to the naturalization of intolerance and violence. The widespread talk of nationalism as a 'substitute religion' ultimately downplays what occurred in Germany during the nineteenth and twentieth centuries, namely the 'Germanization of Christianity'. Where national enemy stereotypes reign, religious toleration is the first casualty. Thus, for the 'Confessing Church', the persecution of the Jews culminating in their deportation became 'a further confirmation of a Jewish destiny already laid down in the Bible', as the church historian Arnold Angenendt summarizes it. The aggressive anti-Semitism of Protestant communities conformed to the anti-Semitism decreed by the state. Accordingly, from 1941 onwards, in many communities Christians wearing the Star of David were even refused admission to services. What has remained insufficiently clarified to this day is the role that the methodological nationalism of the historical sciences and theology played in this. This means that here the Carl Schmitt error still dominates people's thinking. The uniform friend–enemy logic of demarcation is accepted for the nation and for religion and as a consequence the secular and religious alternatives of transnational and interreligious toleration are 'realistically' excluded from the horizon of the possible. In this sense, the nationalism of Protestant theologians imbued the understanding of religion with the theory of the nation and distorted religion in national political terms. This means that to this day the question of the potential of religion to foster toleration, which is so crucial for the twenty-first century, is answered in the negative even by such a reflective theologian as Friedrich Wilhelm Graf without so much as being seriously entertained.

Truth and peace

In a self-destructive civilization, the key theme of violence and toleration culminates in the question: how is interreligious toleration possible? How was it possible to recognize the religious others as other (and not as the same) instead of disparaging them as adversaries of the 'true faith' and robbing them of their religious and human dignity? Here the historical justification of religions in the twenty-first century is related to the concern over the continued existence of humanity.

How is a type of interreligious toleration possible in which brotherly love and confessional enmity are not two sides of belief in God? A type of toleration, therefore, whose goal is not truth but peace?

In the first place, there is Lessing's answer in *Nathan the Wise*. In the parable of the rings Lessing anticipated the contradiction between the one truth and the cosmopolitan recognition of the many religious truths. However, Nathan's wisdom consists in the ruse of not playing truth off against peace but of according both goals – truth *and* peace – equal importance alongside each other. In the words of the parable: both must exist, the unique ring and the many rings each of which must be regarded as the unique ring by the son who inherits it from the father. Thus each ring is the 'unique' ring which does not exist.

Mahatma Gandhi lived this out biographically in that he first learned the world of his own religion through the eyes of others. As a young man Gandhi went to England to study law. This 'detour' into the heartland of the Christian West did not alienate him from Hinduism but deepened his understanding and profession of it. For it was in England that Gandhi began at the invitation of a friend to read the Bhagavad Gita, which was destined to open his eyes – and in an English translation. Only afterwards did he devote himself to the intensive study of the Hindu text in Sanskrit. Thus he was led to discover the spiritual wealth of his own tradition by seeing it through the eyes of his Western friends.

Separating dogma from practice

Heated debates and controversies are being conducted everywhere over the 'problem' of Islam in 'secular' Europe. Hidden beneath the public battles being conducted by religious warriors over demarcation, the cunning of the added value of cooperation is acquiring increasing reality and importance. Groups can be intolerant with regard to the theology of others yet nevertheless cooperate in creative ways to promote shared public concerns (whether of a religious or a more general nature). The theological custodians of dogmas and inveterate militants could learn something from this 'reason of double religion', namely to separate dogma from practice. Thus there are innumerable examples of the successful separation between dogma and practice in communities in the United States, but also in Europe and many other parts of the world. Here the religious groups provide mutual support for the practical concerns of the others, though they also make common cause in matters relating to schools, in combating poverty and exclusion and in support of the integration of (illegal) immigrants.

Europe, and hence also Germany, does not have a (bright) future unless it assimilates the outlook of others. Consider, for example, the simple fact that every fourth child in Germany is growing up under conditions of bi-national parenthood. But one should also consider that all of the greatest European minds, whose names adorn our schools and universities, wrestled with the relation between cosmopolitanism and patriotism, and thus with the inclusion of the outlook of others.

Why is so little attention – either intellectual or political – paid to this classical tradition of the cosmopolitan outlook today in Germany and Europe where we so urgently need it in the globalized world? I don't know the answer to this question.

15

The Caterpillar's Mistake: Fukushima and the End of Nuclear Power*

June 2011

'You Germans are on your own', was the reaction of Stewart Brand, the American environmentalist, to Germany's plans to phase out atomic energy. Brand added that Germany's decision was irresponsible. Economic considerations and the threat represented by greenhouse gases mean that we simply cannot renounce atomic energy. 'I had my doubts, but Fukushima persuaded me of the merits of nuclear power', was George Monbiot's provocative comment. Up to now, there have been no fatalities from the nuclear disaster, even though the reactors in Japan have been subjected to the severest test possible: one of the worst earthquakes ever followed by a tsunami. So Monbiot now loves atomic power.

*I was a member of the special expert commission appointed by Chancellor Merkel in the wake of the Fukushima disaster in Japan. This chapter presents some of the panel's recommendations, which have become the foundation of Mrs Merkel's policy of switching to alternative energy sources by 2021.

It would be utterly mistaken to imagine that Germany's political decision to phase out nuclear power means that it is turning its back on the European concept of modernity in favour of the dark forests, the obscure roots of German intellectual history. This is not simply the latest outburst of Germany's proverbial love of the irrational, but rather proof of its faith in modernity's adaptability and creativity in its dealings with risks which it has itself generated.

Supporters of atomic energy base their judgements on a concept of risk immune to experience, a concept that confuses the period of early industrialization with the nuclear age. Their risk rationale assumes that the worst can happen and that we have to be prepared for it. If the roof is ablaze, the fire brigade arrives, the insurance pays out, and the doctors are there to treat the casualties. Transferred to the risks of nuclear power, this would require that even in the worst-case scenario, the radiation from our uranium would be a hazard for only a few hours rather than for thousands of years, with no need to evacuate the population of any nearby city. This is nonsense. Following Chernobyl and Fukushima, anyone who still maintains that French, British, American or Chinese reactors are safe fails to recognize that, from the weight of the evidence, we ought to draw exactly the opposite conclusion. After all, if anything is clear, it is that another nuclear disaster is a certainty. The only question is where and when it will occur.

There are those who argue that there can be no such thing as risk-free power generation with any large-scale plants, and that is perfectly true. But if they go on to infer that in the clean use of coal, biomass, water, wind, sun and also atomic energy, the risks may vary but are comparable, they are trying to wriggle out of the awkward truth, which is that we are perfectly aware of what happens when there is a nuclear meltdown. We know how long radiation lasts, what effect caesium and iodine have on human beings and the environment and how many generations would have to suffer if the worst actually happened. What is more, we know that these unlimited consequences – spatial, temporal and social – do *not* apply to the alternative, renewable energy sources. Anyone who, like Monbiot, makes the number of fatalities the yardstick of risk obscures the damage done to the unborn and to the evacuees, thereby turning risk analysis into a kind of ideology.

What about insurance? Curiously enough, in the United States, that empire of free-market economics, nuclear power was the first state-socialist industry – at any rate, when it comes to who assumes the costs of mistakes. The profits go into private pockets, while the risks are socialized; in other words, they are transferred to the taxpayer and to future generations. If the nuclear industry were forced to take out disaster insurance, that would spell the end of the myth of cheap nuclear power. The nineteenth-century concept of risk, when applied to nuclear power at the beginning of the twenty-first century, is a zombie concept, a category of the living dead that blinds us to the reality in which we live.

No other industrial nation is going to abandon nuclear power as quickly as Germany. Doesn't that show that this an exaggerated panic reaction? No. It is not the product of German angst. *It's the economy, stupid!* In the long run, nuclear power will become more expensive, while renewable energy will become cheaper. But those who continue to leave all options open will not invest in the latter. A hesitant Germany would fail to achieve the required impetus of a self-fulfilling prophecy in energy change. So one could say that while Germans aren't full of angst, they are driven by a subtle anxiety. They sense the economic opportunities of future global markets. To the Germans, the 'energy revolution' spells jobs. A cynic might say: let other countries pride themselves on their fearlessness regarding nuclear power – it will all end in technical stagnation and wasted investment. Supporters of nuclear power block their own access to the markets of the future because they are not investing in energy-saving products, renewable energy, 'green' professional training and research institutes.

The situation we are facing at the dawn of the twenty-first century is comparable to other turning points in energy production. Just imagine what would have happened 250 years ago if people had brushed aside the suggestion that they should invest in coal and steel, steam engines, power looms and, later on, railways; or what the world would be like now if fifty years ago people had seen the Americans suddenly investing in microprocessors, computers, the Internet, and the new markets that those technologies opened up – and dismissed it all as a product of American angst. We are at a similar crossroads of history today. If we could open up just a part of the deserts for solar energy production, we could satisfy the energy needs of the entire planet. No one can take possession of sunlight; no one can privatize or nationalize it. Everyone can open up this source of energy for himself or herself and profit from it. Some of the poorest countries in the world are 'solar rich'.

Nuclear power is hierarchical and anti-democratic by its very nature. The exact opposite holds true for sources of renewable energy, like the sun and the wind. Users of energy produced by a nuclear power plant have their electricity cut off if they fail to pay their bills. This cannot happen to people using electricity generated by the solar panels installed on the roofs of their houses. Solar energy makes people independent. It is obvious that the availability of solar energy will threaten the monopoly of nuclear power. Why, of all peoples, do the Americans, the French, and the British, who value freedom so highly, persist in remaining blind to the emancipatory consequences of the coming change in power generation?

People everywhere are proclaiming and mourning the death of politics. Paradoxically, the cultural perception of dangers like nuclear catastrophes may well usher in the very opposite: the end of the end of politics. To understand this, we need to return to an insight of John Dewey's, formulated originally as early as 1927, in *The Public and its Problems*. According to Dewey, a transnational public sphere powerful enough to create a community arises not from political decisions but from the consequences of decisions which have come to seem problematic in the lives of citizens. Thus a publicly perceived risk triggers communication among people who would otherwise prefer to have nothing to do with one another. It imposes obligations and costs on people who resist – and who often have the prevailing law on their side. In other words, what is denounced by many as a hysterical overreaction to the 'risks' of nuclear power is in fact a vital step towards ensuring that a turning point in energy generation becomes a step towards greater democracy.

Given the realistic alternatives of renewable energy, the strategies for action opened up by nuclear power's perceived potential for disaster completely disrupt the equilibrium established by the neoliberal alliance between capital and the state. The prospect of a nuclear disaster empowers both states and social movements to develop new sources of legitimation and new courses of action. The novel coalition between the state and social movements, of the kind we currently see at work in Germany, now has a historic opportunity. Even in terms of power politics, this change of policy makes sense. Only a conservative government close to industry is capable of pulling off such a shift in energy policy, since the most vocal opponents are to be found within its own ranks.

It could well be that those who criticize Germany's decision to opt out of nuclear power have fallen victim to the caterpillar's mistake: as it emerges from the chrysalis, it laments the disappearance of the cocoon because it has no premonition of the butterfly of renewable energy that it is destined to become.

16

It's Time to Get Angry, Europe. Create the Europe of Citizens Now!

July 2011

The European common currency is in trouble. Several EU countries are facing mountains of debt and solidarity within the currency bloc is declining. It is European youth, in particular, who have drawn the short straw. Closer cooperation is the only way forward.

Redefining Europe for the twenty-first century

Europe already accomplished a miracle once before: enemies became neighbours. In the light of the euro crisis, the cardinal question must be confronted once again: how can Europe guarantee its citizens peace, freedom and security in the risk storms raging in the globalized world? This calls for nothing less than a second miracle: how can the Europe of bureaucracy become a Europe of citizens?

European policy is about to undergo a transformation as significant as Ostpolitik, the country's improvement of relations with the Soviet bloc, was in the early 1970s. While that policy was characterized by the slogan 'change through rapprochement', the new approach might be dubbed 'more justice through more Europe'.

It is a question of overcoming a divide: between the East and the West in the 1970s and between North and South today. Politicians tirelessly insist that Europe is a community of fate. It has been that way since the establishment of the European Union. The EU is an idea that grew out of the physical and moral devastation following the Second World War. Ostpolitik was an idea dedicated to defusing the Cold War and perforating the Iron Curtain.

Unlike earlier nations and empires that celebrated their origins in myths and heroic victories, the EU is a transnational governmental institution that emerged from the agony of defeat and consternation over the Holocaust. But now that war and peace is no longer the overriding issue, what does the European community of fate signify as a new generational experience? It is the existential threat posed by the financial, debt and currency crisis which is making Europeans realize that they do not live in Germany or France, but in Europe. For the first time, Europe's young people are experiencing their own 'European fate'. Today one in five Europeans under twenty-five is unemployed. Better educated than ever and nourishing high expectations, they are confronting a decline in the labour markets triggered by the threat of national bankruptcies and the economic crisis.

Once upon a time, after the Greek debt had been devalued, people began to breathe easily and to draw hope: Europe had survived and was perhaps even strong and agile enough to overcome its problems. Then the Greek prime minister Giorgios Papandreou announced that he wanted to put the fateful question of the EU rescue package to the Greek people in a referendum. Suddenly, the hidden, inverted reality came to light. In Europe, which is so proud of its democracy, someone who practises democracy becomes a threat to Europe!

Papandreou was forced to call off the democratic referendum.

Whereas just a short time ago we had hoped, to quote the German poet Hölderlin, that 'Where there is danger, salvation grows too', now a new counter-reality is appearing on the horizon: where there is salvation, danger grows too. At any rate, the anxious question has suddenly wormed its way into people's heads: are the measures introduced to rescue the euro abolishing European democracy? Will the 'rescued' EU cease to be a European Union as we know it and instead become an 'EE', a European Empire with a German-French stamp? Are these never-ending crises giving birth to a political monster?

Not long ago it was still commonplace to speak in disparaging terms about the cacophony in the European Union. Now all of a sudden Europe has *a single* telephone. It rings in Berlin and for the moment it belongs to Angela Merkel.

Yesterday it seemed as though the crises were raising the old question of the *finalité* of European unification: should Europe become a nation writ large, a confederation, a federal state, a mere economic community, an informal United Nations or something historically new – namely, a cosmopolitan Europe founded on European law which performs the task of politically coordinating Europeanized nation states? All of that suddenly looks like folklore from times past. Even asking 'Which Europe do we want?' is to act as though one could still choose one option or the other.

The Greek government, which has to demand the most of its citizens, is in effect under guardianship and, in view of the domestic disturbances, has its back to the wall. Debt liquidation specialists are in demand – for example, Mario Monti and Lucas Papademos. For the austerity packages have proved to be suicide programmes for the governments of the debtor nations, which were promptly elected out of office. The Irish and Portuguese governments were the first to suffer this fate, followed by the Greek, Italian and Spanish governments.

Not only has the power structure undergone a permanent shift. Instead, a new logic of power is taking shape. Remarkably enough, Max Weber included a brief excursus on the concept of the 'Empire State' in his sociology of domination (though its main focus was on the state). 'Even without any formal power of command', Weber wrote, an Empire State 'can exercise a far-reaching and occasionally even a despotic hegemony.' As examples he cited the role of Prussia in the German Customs Union and the status of New York 'as the seat of the great financial powers'. Must Germany's role in crisis-ridden Europe now be added to this list?

This is what the new Europe looks like: the grammar of power conforms to the imperial difference between creditor and debtor countries. Thus it is not a military but an economic logic. (In this respect the talk of the 'Fourth Reich' is wide of the mark.) Its ideological foundation is German euro-nationalism, that is, an extended European version of Deutschmark nationalism (see chapter 10, "German Euro-Nationalism"). In this way the German culture of stability is being elevated into the guiding idea for Europe. The stabilization of hegemonic power rests on the assent of the dependent European countries. Some Germans do believe that the German model exerts a magnetic power of attraction on the people of Europe: Europe is learning German, they say. But it is more realistic to ask: what is the basis of the power of enforcement? Angela Merkel has dictated that the price for incurring debt without restraint is the loss of sovereignty.

The consequence is the splitting of the EU. This is reflected, first, in the new internal conflict between the euro countries and the EU countries outside the euro zone. Those who do not have the euro find themselves excluded from the decision-making processes which are shaping the present and future of Europe. They find themselves degraded to onlookers and are losing their political voice. This is most apparent in the case of Great Britain, which is sliding into European irrelevance.

However, a dramatic split is also occurring in the new, crisis-torn centre of activity of the euro countries, a split between the countries which already or will soon depend on the drip feed of the rescue fund and the countries which are financing the rescue fund. The former have no alternative but to submit to the claim to power of German euro-nationalism. Italy, perhaps one of the most European countries, is in danger of playing no further role in shaping the present and future of the continent.

My point is not just that the euro crisis is tearing Europe apart. That is no doubt true. But the crux of the matter is that in the process the basic rules of European democracy are being suspended or are even being inverted into their opposite, bypassing parliaments, governments and EU institutions. Multilateralism is turning into unilateralism, equality into hegemony, sovereignty into the deprivation of sovereignty and recognition into disrespect for the democratic dignity of other nations. Even France, which long dominated European unification, must submit to Berlin's strictures now that it must fear for its international credit rating.

In fact, this future, which is taking shape in the laboratory of the euro rescue as an intentional side-effect, as it were, resembles – I hesitate to say it – a belated European variant of the Soviet Union. In this case, a centralized planned economy no longer means five-year plans for goods and services, but five-year plans for debt reduction. The power to implement them is being placed in the hands of 'commissioners' who are authorized by 'rights of direct access' (Merkel) to stop at nothing in tearing down the Potemkin villages erected by notorious debtor countries. We all know how the USSR ended.

Why must it now be a German Europe after all, something which the German writer Thomas Mann already warned urgently against? Without Europe, Germany cannot be German. Even the reunification of the two Germanies was made possible only by the project of constructing a European peace order. In the euro crisis, too, what is (or should become) 'German' and what 'European' are becoming mixed in new ways. Germany is too sovereign, powerful, European and economically interconnected to be able to enjoy the luxury of not rescuing the euro. An elephant doesn't inspire confidence by pretending to be a dove. Thus the road leading to the EE is once again paved with good European intentions. Those involved are always at pains to replace the German taboo word 'power' with 'responsibility', the Germans' favourite word.

Angela Merkel spells out 'European responsibility' in accordance with the maxims of power governing German euro-nationalism. This means that German answers must be sought to the European crisis; indeed the German culture of stability must ultimately provide the master key to a broader European answer to the European crisis. In this way a mixture of authentic commitment to Europe and genuine nationalism has arisen, a mixture of more or less feigned commitment to Europe for foreign consumption, but also of more or less feigned nationalism for the swelling ranks of Eurosceptics among the Germans. This is an attempt to reconcile the irreconcilable on the basis of power pragmatism: to rescue the euro and the EU *and* to win elections against the background of an anti-European mood in Germany.

The chancellor is cutting European values down to national size: internally democracy, externally 'losers can't be choosers'. The magic formula of post-war Germany, 'stability policy', means once again renouncing political freedom – in this case, the freedom of others. In a mixture of high-minded confusion, hypocrisy,

Protestant severity and European calculation peculiar to Merkel, the Merkel government is elevating German euro-nationalism into the guiding principle for intervening in the economic policy of the offending countries. At stake is nothing less than civilizing the debt-mad South – in the name of 'economic reason', 'Europe' and the 'world economy'. Here the slogan is: The more European our fiscal policy is, the more German it becomes.

However, the self-obstruction of the EU could diminish in the shadow of this hegemonic structure – it could! In fact, the question of how this enormous space comprising twenty-seven member states should be governed if, before every decision, twenty-seven heads of government, cabinets and parliaments have to be convinced, has answered itself, as it were. In contrast to the EU, the euro zone is *de facto* a community of two speeds. In future only the euro zone (not the EU) will belong to the avant-garde of Europeanization. This could represent an opportunity for the urgently needed institutional imagination.

There has long been talk of an 'economic government'. What is behind this needs to be fleshed out, negotiated and tested. Sooner or later the highly controversial euro bonds will also be introduced. The German finance minister, Wolfgang Schäuble, is already arguing for the introduction of a tax on financial transactions which, in the larger EU, would founder on Britain's veto.

Yet this path leading to a Europe of apparatchiks – a Brussels or Berlin politburo – is the completion of the birth defect of the organized Europe and pushes the paradox of a really existing Europe without Europeans to an extreme. Even more, the citizens of the lender nations think that they are being fleeced, the citizens of the borrower nations that they are being disenfranchised. For both, Europe is turning into the enemy. Instead of a Europe of citizens, an angry civic movement against Europe is taking shape.

Create the Europe of citizens now!

US President John F. Kennedy once astonished the world with his idea to create a Peace Corps. By analogy, the neo-European Angela Merkel could surprise the world with the insight and initiative that the Euro crisis is not just about the economy but about initiating the Europeanization of Europe from below, about diversity and self-determination, about a political and cultural space in which the citizens no longer confront each other as enemies who have been disenfranchised or fleeced. Create the Europe of citizens now!

The talk of 'enlargement' and 'deepening' would as a result acquire a new meaning. What would have to be enlarged and deepened would be democracy in Europe. The rule of law and the market are not sufficient. Freedom needs a third pillar if it is to become secure; its name is European civil society or, in more concrete terms, *doing Europe* or European civic activity. Such an autonomous civic practice, providing basic funding for Europe's unemployed youth, would doubtlessly cost a pile of money, though only a fraction of the zeros which have already been, and are probably going to be, swallowed up by the rescue of the banks.

Have no fear of direct democracy! Without transnational opportunities for interventions from below, without European referenda on European themes which send a shudder through the ocean liner Europe, the whole enterprise will fail. Why not elect the president of the European commission directly in an election involving all European citizens on the same day – which would therefore be European in the strict sense for the first time? It might also make sense to appoint a new constitutional convention, which this time would confer democratic legitimation on another Europe – let us call it the 'European Community of Democracies' (ECD). That would be a beginning, not the answer to the European crisis.

At stake is the opposition of social-human reason to self-destructive risk capitalism, the kind of opposition which the philosopher Ernst Bloch once called 'pacifism of strength', in contrast to a 'pacifism of weakness' which he described as a 'familiar mixture of lemonade and platitude'. If one really wants to spell this future enfranchisement out in European terms, then the saccharine-sweet formula of 'European understanding' is not sufficient. We have to speak in terms of the Europe of the '*citoyen*', the 'citizen', the '*burgermaatschappij*', the '*ciudadano*', the '*opywatel*'; thus of the antagonisms hidden in the unifying formula 'Europe of the citizens'. For it is a well-known fact that each of these national cultural key concepts stands for a different path to political modernity, hence for a different historical horizon of experience and memory, which to this day profoundly shapes the understanding of democracy, the political institutions and cultures of the European states.

The cosmopolitan European democracy which binds the national democracies cannot be a national democracy. How is a European democracy possible without disenfranchising the national parliaments? Assuming that one recognizes that implementing democratic rights involves and requires many paths, arms, channels and guarantees – supranational, transnational, national and local – can the democratic empowerment of a cosmopolitan Europe be accompanied by a strengthening of its national democracies in the member states?

The answer has to be that the new Europe would not follow the model of German euro-nationalism but would be an emerging European Community of Democracies. And sharing sovereignty becomes a multiplier of power and democracy.

17

Powerless but Legitimate: The Occupy Movement in the Financial Crisis

---

August 2011

How is it possible that a hot American autumn is following the model of the Arab by launching an assault on the founding faith of the West, the economic conception of the world embodied in the 'American way of life'? How is it possible that the call to 'Occupy Wall Street' is mobilizing young people not only in other US states but also in London and Vancouver, Brussels and Rome, Frankfurt and Tokyo?

And the protesters are not assembling just to raise their voices against a bad law or for a particular cause but against 'the system' as such. What was recently known as 'free-market economy' and now again as 'capitalism', is being placed under the microscope and being exposed to fundamental criticism. Why is the world suddenly willing to pay attention when 'Occupy Wall Street' claims to speak for the ninety-nine per cent of those who have been overrun against the one per cent of profiteers?

On the website WeAreThe99Percent one can read the personal experiences of the ninety-nine per cent: of those who have lost their homes in the property crisis, those who form the new underclass; of those who cannot afford health insurance and those who have to take out loans in order to be able to study. It is not the 'superfluous' (Zygmunt Bauman), the excluded, the proletariat, but people from the mainstream of society who are protesting in the public squares. This is delegitimizing and destabilizing 'the system'. The *citoyen* is making a comeback across the globe!

To be sure, the global financial risk is not (yet) a global financial disaster. But it could become one. This catastrophic subjunctive is the typhoon which, in the shape of the financial crisis, has struck at the heart of the social institutions and people's everyday lives – irregular, beyond the domain of the constitution and democracy, explosively charged with unacknowledged non-knowing and sweeping away established points of orientation.

At the same time this is lending concrete form to a kind of community of fate among the ninety-nine per cent. Indications of this are the abrupt slumps in the financial graphs whose rollercoaster rides are rendering global connections tangible. If Greece goes bankrupt, is that further evidence that my pension in Germany is no longer secure? What does 'government default' even mean? For me?

Who would have thought that conceited banks, no less, would come begging for assistance from cash-strapped states? And who would have thought that these states, with their chronically empty pockets, would make astronomical sums of money available in short order to the cathedrals of capitalism? Today everyone is aware of this kind of thing – which doesn't mean that anyone understands it.

This anticipation of global financial risk reaching into the capillaries of everyday life is one of the great mobilizations of the twenty-first century. For everywhere this kind of threat is perceived locally as a cosmopolitan event giving rise to an existentialist short circuit between one's own country and the lives of everyone else.

Such events clash with the conceptual and institutional framework in terms of which we have comprehended society and politics until now. They place this framework in question from within, but at the same time confront highly diverse cultural, economic and political assumptions and backgrounds. The global protest assumes correspondingly diverse local forms.

The financial flows – but by no means all commercial relations and conditions of production in the economy, only these new digital financial transactions circulating around the entire planet in real time, which can carry along whole countries only to let them come crashing down – point in an exemplary way to the new kind of protest dynamic in world risk society.

For the globalized financial risks represent a kind of objective demonstration of the conditions against themselves. Under the dictate of necessity, people are being subjected to a kind of crash course on the contradictions of financial capitalism in the world risk society. The reporting in the mass media is revealing the radical separation between those who produce the risks and profit from them and those who have to suffer their consequences.

In the country of predatory capitalism, the United States, the movement critical of capitalism is taking shape – another incredible moment. We said 'madness' when the Berlin Wall collapsed. We said 'madness' when the Twin Towers in New York disintegrated in a heap of dust on 11 September 2001. And we said 'madness' when the global financial crisis erupted with the collapse of Lehman Brothers.

What is this 'madness'? First, there are the sudden conversions worthy of a comedy revue: bankers and managers, the absolute market fundamentalists, are calling for state aid. Politicians like Angela Merkel and Peer Steinbrück in Germany, who recently were cheerleaders for unregulated capitalism, have changed opinion and sides under cover of darkness to a kind of state socialism for the rich.

And everywhere non-knowing holds sway. Nobody knows what is going on and the actual effects of the therapy prescribed in a sudden rush of zeros to the head. All of us – the ninety-nine per cent – are part of a large-scale economic experiment. This is being conducted, on the one hand, in the fictional space of more or less unacknowledged non-knowing, because something which must not occur under any circumstances is to be prevented, both as regards the means employed as well as the hoped-for goals; on the other hand, it is an experiment with brutal consequences for everyone.

One can distinguish between different types of revolutions: coups d'état, class struggles, civil disobedience, and so forth. The global financial threats do not conform to any of these models. They are instead the politically explosive embodiment of the errors of the neoliberal financial capitalism which was still dominant until recently and which, with the violence of its victory march and the accompanying looming catastrophe, now demands that these threats be acknowledged and corrected. They are a kind of collective return of the repressed: the neoliberal self-confidence is being reproached with its own mistakes.

To be sure, economic crises are as old as the markets themselves and since the global financial crisis of 1929, at the latest, it is common knowledge that financial collapses can have disastrous consequences – for politics in particular.

The Bretton Woods institutions established after the Second World War were conceived in this sense as global political answers to global economic problems, and the fact that they functioned was a key factor in the emergence of the European welfare state.

But since the 1970s, and even more so since the collapse of the Communist competitor in the East, these regulating institutions have been largely dismantled and replaced by sequential ad hoc solutions. The global financial risks which are jeopardizing the situation of people throughout the world are giving rise to new 'involuntary' forms of politicization. This is what constitutes their – political and intellectual – dynamism.

Globality means that everyone is affected by these risks and everyone also sees himself or herself as being affected. It would be over-hasty to conclude that this is already giving rise to joint action. But there is something like an awareness of crisis fuelled by the risk which represents precisely this kind of common threat, a new kind of collective fate.

The outcry of the 'ninety-nine per cent' shows that world risk society can achieve a reflective conception of itself at a cosmopolitan moment. That becomes possible when the objective demonstration of the conditions against themselves allows itself to be transformed into political commitment, into a global Occupy movement, in which those who have been overrun, the frustrated and the fascinated – hence potentially everyone – actually or virtually take to the streets.

But what is the source of the power or powerlessness of the Occupy movement? The fact that even stock exchange sharks are declaring their solidarity with each other is not enough. The global financial risk and its political and social consequences have stripped neoliberal capitalism of its legitimacy. The result is an asymmetry of power and legitimacy.

There is a surplus of power and a dearth of legitimacy on the side of capital and the states and a dearth of power and high legitimacy on the side of the carnivalesque protesters. That is an imbalance which the Occupy movement could use to press home its core demands – for example, a global tax on financial transactions – in the enlightened self-interest of the nation states and against their own narrow-mindedness.

Implementing this Robin Hood tax would give rise to an exemplary, legitimate and powerful alliance between global protest movements and national politics which could accomplish the political quantum leap into a situation in which state actors are able to act transnationally within and beyond national borders. If even German Chancellor Angela Merkel and French President Nicolas Sarkozy are now at least paying lip service to this key demand, then one can attest this goal at least a chance of being realized.

To generalize, global awareness of risk – that is, the anticipation of disasters which must be prevented at all costs – is opening up a new field of political power. The alliance between global protest movements and national politics could ensure in the long term that democracy dominates the economy rather than the economy dominating democracy. An Occupy movement that sets itself goals capable of achieving internal and external consensus could bring this golden opportunity within reach. This would go beyond merely monitoring the banking sector to include fair taxation policy and social security on a transnational scale.

The following insight might be helpful against the reflex to condemn this as 'hopeless': the chief adversaries of the global financial sector are not those who are at the moment pitching their tents on the public squares and before the cathedrals of finance across the world, however important and indispensable they may be. The most convincing and tenacious opponent of the global financial sector – is the global financial sector itself.

18

Cooperate or Bust! The Existential Crisis of the European Union

September 2011

When a world-order collapses, then the analysis begins, though that doesn't seem to hold for the type of social theory currently prevalent. With universalist aloofness and somnambulant certainty, it hovers above the currents of epochal change: global warming, financial crises and the crisis of democracy and national institutions. Today this kind of universalist social analysis, whether it be structuralist, interactionist, Marxist or based on critical or systems theory, is antiquated and provincial: antiquated because it excludes what is patent, namely, a paradigm shift in modern society and politics; provincial because it falsely absolutizes the path-dependent scope of experience and expectation in Western European and American modernization, thus distorting the sociological view of its particularity.

It would be an understatement to say that European sociology needs to understand the modernization of other societies for supplementary reasons, in order to complete its worldview. It is rather the case that we Europeans can understand ourselves only if we 'deprovincialize' – in other words, if we learn to see through the eyes of others as a matter of sociological method. This is what I call the cosmopolitan turn in sociological and political theory and research.

The paradigmatic case I would like to use to explain this cosmopolitan turn is the existential crisis of the European Union in the era of cosmopolitization.

I will develop the argument in three stages. First: what does 'cosmopolitization' – as opposed to 'cosmopolitanism' – mean? Why is it so essential that the social sciences should discuss 'cosmopolitization' (and not 'globalization')? Second: how far is a new perspective on the current European crisis opened up by the cosmopolitan turn and the facts of cosmopolitization? Third: what methodological consequences can be inferred? What does cosmopolitization mean in terms of sociological research? How can the currently predominant 'methodological nationalism' be replaced by 'methodological cosmopolitanism'?

1. What is meant by 'cosmopolitization'?

We are living in an era not of cosmopolitanism but of cosmopolitization: the 'global other' is in our midst. The concept of cosmopolitization is surrounded by misunderstandings and misinterpretations. The best way to make it comprehensible is through a paradigmatic example: that of global transplant medicine. The victory of global transplant surgery (and not its crisis!) has swept away its own ethical foundations and paved the way for a shadow economy that supplies the world market with 'fresh' organs. In a radically unequal world, there is clearly no shortage of desperate individuals prepared to sell a kidney, a section of their liver, a lung, an eye, even a testicle for a pittance. The destinies of patients waiting for organs in the centre are linked in obscure ways with the destinies of the destitute on the peripheries: both groups are contending with problems of immediate survival. This gives rise to what I call a really existing cosmopolitization of emergency.

In a fascinating case study, the anthropologist Nancy Scheper-Hughes has shown how the excluded of the world, the economically and politically disenfranchised – refugees, the homeless, street children, paperless migrants, ageing prostitutes, cigarette smugglers and thieves – feel forced to sell their organs. They are thereby physically, morally and economically 'incorporated' into the mortally ill bodies of other people, people wealthy enough to purchase the organs of the global poor and to have their bodies 'surgically patched up' with them.

Continents, 'races', classes, nations and religions merge in the cosmopolitized, corporeal landscape of the individual. Muslim kidneys clean Christian blood. White racists breathe with the help of black lungs. The blond manager looks at the world with the eye of an African street child. A secular millionaire survives thanks to the liver cut out of a Protestant prostitute in a Brazilian favela. The bodies of the rich become patchwork quilts. The poor, in contrast, are maimed, becoming actual or potential one-eyed or one-kidneyed depositories of spare parts, 'of their own free will' and 'in their own interests', as the wealthy sick repeat to themselves like a litany. The piecemeal sale of their organs is their life insurance. At the other end of the line evolves the biopolitical 'world citizen' – a white, male body, fit or fat, with an Indian kidney or a Muslim eye.

Generally speaking, the traffic in living kidneys follows existing flows of capital from South to North, from poor to wealthy bodies, from black and brown bodies to white, from women to men and from poor men to richer men. Women are rarely the beneficiaries of purchased organs. The age of cosmopolitization is thus divided into organ-selling and organ-buying nations. The global poor is in our corporeal midst – and for that reason alone is no longer a 'global other'.

WikiLeaks as cosmopolitan subpolitics

The preceding example is a perfect illustration of the following: cosmopolitization signifies the basic facts of the *conditio humana* at the beginning of the twenty-first century. The dualisms into which the first, nationally organized modernity was ordered and understood have, after the victory of universalized modernization processes (in this case transplant surgery), been dissolved and re-fused. This holds for the dualisms of national and international, us and them, inside and outside, as well as for the binaries nature and society, centre and periphery.

WikiLeaks, for example, in an act of cosmopolitan subpolitics has completely undermined the basic distinction between 'secret' and 'not secret', causing enormous turbulence within the world of the nation states, overturning their hierarchies and destabilizing the geographical, historical and economic situation of individual states.

These facts of cosmopolitization are certainly a concern of the social sciences, and therefore it is important to distinguish clearly between philosophical cosmopolitanism and sociological cosmopolitanism.

Cosmopolitanism, in the philosophical sense of Immanuel Kant and Jürgen Habermas, means something active, a task, a conscious decision, one which is clearly the responsibility of an elite and is implemented from above. Today, on the other hand, a banal, forced and 'impure' cosmopolitization is unfolding powerfully and aggressively beneath the surface, involuntary and unnoticed, behind the façade of existing national spaces, sovereign territories and customs. It reaches from the top of society down to the everyday life of the family, affecting work situations, individual careers and bodies, even though national flags are still waved and national attitudes, identities and forms of consciousness are even growing stronger.

Let us take another, only apparently extreme example: the cosmopolitization of the village. In practically every country in the Far East (though in Europe, too), farmers are emerging as the biggest losers of 'compressed modernization'. At first glance, most East Asian villages might appear relatively stable and well off; however, they have seen an unprecedented exodus of inhabitants, especially young women. Paradoxically, migration from the countryside has given rise to fundamental new facts and categories of the 'cosmopolitan marriage and family', and thus the 'cosmopolitan village'. Like the sudden arrival of American and Japanese colonial masters in Korean villages in the early twentieth century, the unexpected appearance of 'foreign brides' has forced today's villagers to expose themselves to the experience of foreign worlds: the global other lives and loves in our midst – and by no means only in the urban centres.

2. What is meant by the cosmopolitization of Europe?

The facts of cosmopolitization affect first of all what sociology refers to as 'intermediary institutions', in other words, the family, the household ('global care chains'), the workplace (since new processes of production relativize or even annul national organizational borders of production, thereby involuntarily producing a cosmopolitization of territorially fixed Western centres of employment), the village, the banal, everyday cosmopolitization of foodstuffs, and, finally, the cosmopolitization of art, science, religion, and so on.

All in all, it's clear that one cannot study the historical facts of cosmopolitization only at the meso-level of intermediary institutions, but that one also needs to look at the micro and macro levels; cosmopolitization, in other words, permeates the major fields of communication, interaction and social and political practices. This brings me to my key subject: reflexive Europeanization.

First of all, however, what do we mean by Europe?

If one attempts to examine Europe more closely, either in political terms or in terms of social science, one ends up in a hall of mirrors. Europe expands or contracts depending on one's perspective; the slightest movement and its proportions are distorted. Where it begins and where it ends, what it is and what it should be – there are no straightforward and unambiguous answers to these questions. Whether one equates Europe with the European Union and its member states, or means a larger geographical and political space, including Russia and Belarus, for example – Europe *per se* doesn't exist, there is only Europeanization, understood as an institutional-ized process of ongoing transformation. What 'Europe' includes and excludes, where and how its territorial boundaries run, what institutional forms this Europe possesses and what institutional architecture it should possess in the future – none of this has been defined. Europe is not a fixed state of being. Europe is another word for a variable geometry, variable national interests, variable states of disruption, variable relations towards internal and external factors, variable forms of statehood, variable identity. This also holds for the institutionalized core of Europeanization, the European Union.

The EU as the counter-image of nation state organization

On a first approach, Europe seems to be merely the counter-image to nation state organization: the EU is not a nation writ large, a super-state in which all other nation states are sublimated. The highly particular, historically specific 'power' of the EU, which is not yet fully understood, resides, for example, in the fact that even non-member states that want to become member states (e.g. Turkey) are undergoing processes of internal reform. In short, Europe is not a pre-existing spatial shell within which 'Europeanization' can unfold, nor does there exist a conceptual model or a historical example of the end to which this process is leading.

We are witnessing this in the euro crisis. When the euro was introduced, many economists smugly warned that introducing the currency union without having established a political union was putting the cart before the horse. They couldn't or didn't want to understand that this was precisely the intention! The idea was that the euro and the predictable political problems, through the force of material interest, would compel governments and nations in thrall to national egoisms to extend the political union – following the cosmopolitan imperative: 'cooperate or bust!'

Europe as a market has indeed been one of the contributing factors to the financial and budgetary crisis (witness Ireland), while climate change and financial risks are progressively devaluing the institutional instruments of the EU. Until now, the EU has not offered an institutionalized response. In other words, the EU cannot act – and the political initiatives for dealing with the crisis now lie entirely with the national governments. A more precise description of this situation is necessary, of course.

New power relations have emerged in the current crisis of risk. At crucial moments, it is not the European Commission which acts, nor the EU president, nor the President of the Council of Ministers. In serious cases the ones who decide are the German Chancellor Angela Merkel and the French President Nicolas Sarkozy. Didn't Helmut Kohl, when he introduced the programme of his 1991-4 government, declare that 'Germany is our fatherland, Europe our future'? And didn't Willy Brandt, during the first meeting of the federal German parliament, state: 'German and European belong together now and hopefully for evermore'? The national-economic turn that Angela Merkel has given this avowal has touched a raw nerve, not only among Germany's neighbours. Where Europe is concerned, Angela Merkel acts like Angela Bush. Just as the US president used the risk of terror to thrust the unilateralism of his 'war on terror' upon the rest of the world, so Angela Bush is using the European financial risk to thrust German stability policy unilaterally upon the rest of Europe.

The post-war German model embodied high modern foreign policy: postnational, multilateral, highly peaceful in all areas, preaching interdependence in all directions, everywhere seeking friends, nowhere suspecting enemies; 'power' was almost a dirty word, to be replaced by 'responsibility'; national interests remained, with good reason, always discreetly hidden, like a Biedermeier console, under a heavy tablecloth embroidered with the words 'Europe', 'Peace', 'Collaboration', 'Stability', 'Normality', even 'Humanity'.

Is it really the case, or does it just seem, that the united Europe referred to in the preamble to the German constitution is no longer the guiding star either of German politics or of Germany's self-understanding? The question remains open. What is clear, however, is that Europe is currently confronted with the inadequacy of its institutions. What has also recently become clear is that a Europe without a European fiscal and economic policy is a recipe for disaster.

Europe viewed from without

Perspectives on the cosmopolitization of Europe have thus far ignored (and I mean this self-critically) the question of the influence of de-colonization on the emergence and subsequent development of the European Union. Here, too, it is the victories of modern, industrial capitalism and its effects – global risks, crises and geopolitical shifts, especially since 1989 – that call into question the bases of nation state orders both inside and outside Europe.

From the perspective of the developing countries, however, the current picture of Europe is a somewhat different one. It is informed by a shift in power in favour of postcolonial, developing countries (reflected in their participation in the new G-20 meetings, for example); a shift in the global economic geography of power from the Atlantic to the Pacific; and the steady de-monopolization of the US dollar as the leading global currency in favour of a conglomeration of different currencies and bilateral currency treaties. In addition, there is the growing importance of South–South and East–South partnerships for solving economic problems, not to mention the loss of moral authority and exemplariness of the former Euro-American centre.

The result is that old, Western-dominated centre–periphery models are in danger of collapsing. In the future, things will not revolve primarily around the relation between postcolonialism and Europe. More pertinent will be the extent to which we are witnessing the beginning of a kind of 'precolonialization' of the former centre, Europe, by its former colonies, in particular China and India.

3. From the critique of methodological nationalism to the alternative of methodological cosmopolitanism

The new facts of Europe's postcolonial cosmopolitization will come into focus only when the narrow-mindedness of the still prevailing methodological nationalism is overcome.

Methodological nationalism assumes that nation, state and society are 'natural' social and political forms of the modern world. It assumes a 'natural' division of humanity into a limited number of nations that organize themselves from within and demarcate themselves externally by drawing boundaries between themselves and other nations. It goes still further to represent this external demarcation, in connection with the competition between nation states, as the central category of political organization. Indeed, all sociological thought until now, perhaps even the sociological imagination, has been in thrall to the nation state. Precisely this methodological nationalism prevents the social sciences from shifting the focus of the analysis to the process of cosmopolitization in general and Europeanization in particular.

Where social actors cling to this belief, I speak of a 'national perspective'; where it determines the outlook of social scientists, I speak of 'methodological nationalism'. Methodological nationalism is not a superficial problem or a cosmetic error. It affects the process of data collection and generation as well as the basic concepts of modern sociology and political science, concepts such as 'society', 'social inequality', 'family', 'work', 'religion', 'state', 'democracy' and 'imagined communities'.

A key question raised by methodological cosmopolitanism is: how can units of study be found and defined outside the framework of methodological nationalism that allow the complex processes and (inter)dependencies of cosmopolitization to be understood and analysed in comparative terms? What can be the object of social scientific analysis if, on the one hand, one liberates it from the container of the nation state, but, on the other hand, wants to avoid having recourse to the abstract concepts of the 'world society'?

Recent empirical research in disciplines as diverse as sociology, ethnology, anthropology, geography and political science have developed a large number of concepts all of which aim to break with the supposedly 'natural' equation between 'society/nation/state'. Paul Gilroy's concept of the 'Black Atlantic', Saskia Sassen's identification of the 'global city', Arjun Appadurai's notion of 'scapes', Martin Albrow's concept of the 'global age', and my own analysis of the 'cosmopolitan Europe' are just some examples of research in this direction.

Especially pertinent for methodological cosmopolitanism is the question of the importance of the national and the nation state in defining units of study. Methodologically speaking, the most radical option is to replace the national frame of the unit of study with other foci ('replacing the national'). However, if one were to reduce methodological cosmopolitanism in this way, one would unduly limit its scope and its applicability. Empirical globalization research has long since shown that, in the global era, the nation state does not disappear entirely, and that its value even increases.

The EU as 'lame duck'

A perfect exemplification of this is the global financial risks that have caused a devaluation of the institutional instruments of the EU. The EU has become a 'lame duck' only able to grow new wings through the European initiatives of national governments, in particular Germany and France. It is worthwhile, therefore, to consider the possibility that the nation state will continue to exist, even though it will lose its epistemological monopoly. The methodological task would now be to find new units of study in which the national is contained, but which are no longer one and the same thing as the national. This embedding of the national in processes of cosmopolitization can occur in a variety of ways. The new units of study developed in this variant of methodological cosmopolitanism are correspondingly wide-ranging. One example is the concept of the 'transnational political regime'. This refers to new forms of transnational institution-building which have emerged in connection with a series of problems of global regulation. These institutions organize transnational interactions whose borders are not defined through national sovereignty. They thereby integrate very different and extremely variable groups of actors (public and private) and extend across a variety of territorial levels. These political regimes are often the most appropriate unit of study for an empirical analysis of transnational political regimes.

Crucial here is that these new institutions do not replace the nation state but instead integrate it. Nation states are embedded in new transnational systems of regulation; one of the most important tasks of empirical research is to analyse the specific significance that they acquire in the framework of these institutions. Where the nation state continues to be dominant, as one can regularly observe in international climate politics, whether in Copenhagen or in Cancún, then the transnational level is in danger of degenerating into a mere 'theatre' of the national.

Political consequences

Two insights are unavoidable: first, that national politics in the global era can only regain sovereignty, credibility and the ability to shape events if they assume the form of transnational cooperation – witness the EU as the prime example of this. National sovereignty cannot be won back nationally, but only globally.

Second, if the EU collapses, then the EU member states will also be endangered. There cannot be a politically strong Germany, let alone an export and economic miracle, without the EU. Therefore, more, not less, reflexive Europeanization is in the national and the

European interests of the European nation states. Only then can they avoid their own collapse, which they themselves have provoked with the crisis of the euro.

Perhaps things will move in this direction after all: in times of crisis, it is the euro that protects us, insofar as it forces us to increase cooperation and thereby brings us forward. Even the German Chancellor Angela Merkel now seems to have recognized this ('If the euro fails, then Europe fails too'). And after the crisis we will need more Europe again in order to overcome the next crisis – always following the cosmopolitical imperative: cooperate or bust!

19

What Is Meant by Global Domestic Politics?

The concept 'global domestic politics' and the reality it describes – aren't they a pure illusion? Do they proclaim a new ideology? Do they imply the notion of the world-wide spread of wealth and security? Does global domestic politics mean that everyone is a cosmopolitan if, in their own corner of the global rubbish dump, they see the same advertisements for the same product as billions of other people throughout the world?

Here 'global domestic politics' does not have the meaning of a normative concept in philosophy and political theory but refers instead to a rampantly spreading, wild reality above, below and between the national borders which continue to dominate minds and institutions. Such a new global domestic political wilderness cannot be arrived at deductively (as an inference from a normative philosophy) but must instead be discovered and explored from below, from the mole perspective. The result is the venture of, and the form assumed by, the *Twenty Observations on a World in Turmoil*: curious, angry, provocative, exemplary traces of the future, written between 2009 and 2011. Separating the wheat from the chaff, deciding what will turn out to be transitory and what will remain, is now also a matter for the reader.

In order to assemble elements of a provisional conceptual analysis, it makes sense first to review briefly the observations on a world in turmoil.

1. Mushrooms and Other Flowers of Capitalism

They are the most expensive mushrooms in the world, Japanese matsutake. Their cultivation reflects the outsourcing of environmental risks and at the same time of human beings. And it is legal to boot.

2. All Aboard the Nuclear Power Superjet – Just Don't Ask about the Landing Strip

Climate change and the oil crisis are being used to project atomic energy as a green panacea. In fact, it is a reckless gamble.

3. This Appalling Injustice!

Our reproach to our parents was: how could you have known nothing about the atrocities of the Nazis?! Today thousands are dying on the frontiers of the EU and millions of children are starving to death every day. But we look away. That is at once trivial and deeply outrageous.

4. Harm in Exchange for Money

If man-made climate change has gone beyond the point of no return, if terrorists have access to atomic weapons, if the global economy has already imploded, then every political measure comes too late.

5. Illegal World Citizens

Globalization teaches us that the boastful humanity of the West presupposes inhumanity in dealings with 'illegal' immigrants.

6. The Cards of Power Are Being Reshuffled across the World

The struggle over climate and financial policy is a struggle over a refounding of the political, a cosmopolitan legal system. Nobody knows whether it can succeed.

7. Felt Peace and Waged War

7,200 Bundeswehr soldiers are involved in military operations abroad, and to date eighty-three have died. No statistic – at any rate, no official statistic – is being conducted on the number of those killed by German soldiers.

8. The Return of Social Darwinism or: Which University Do We Want?

The Bologna process has failed. The result is that a new educational catastrophe is looming. Bologna could destroy the universities in their traditional, successful sense.

9. A Kind of Berlin Wall Has Again Collapsed

For weeks a conflict raged over the purchase of 'stolen' Swiss bank data by the German federal or state governments. Then Switzerland renounced an element of national (il)legal sovereignty.

10. *German Euro-Nationalism*

The politicians do not miss any opportunity to miss an opportunity – or so it seems. And the same holds for Pope Benedict XVI.

11. *Beyond the Aeroplane*

The Eyjafjallajökull ash cloud has made the world the gift of a magnificent 'critical experiment': what happens when the flights are cancelled in the air travel society? 'The volcanic cloud came out of the clear blue sky', it was claimed – just like the financial crisis.

12. *Global Domestic Politics from Below: How Global Families Are Becoming Normal*

The family has long since become a crime scene in global domestic politics: fertilization in the Netherlands, pregnancy by an Indian surrogate mother, social mother in Germany – in this way motherhood can degenerate into a legal obstacle race.

13. *The Environmental Storm on the Bastille*

The oil disaster in the Gulf of Mexico is bringing many truths to light. There is the incompetence and indifference demonstrated by the oil company and at the same time the failure of the public controllers. Who would have thought it? The abbreviation 'BP' stands for 'Beyond Petroleum' – the era after oil.

14. *Without Buddha I Could Not Be a Christian*

What seems to be 'religious promiscuity' within the horizon of the ecclesiastical monopoly on the truth could in fact ground the so urgently needed interreligious toleration. Cosmopolitans are in this sense multiple converts.

15. The Caterpillar's Mistake: Fukushima and the End of Nuclear Power

Those who criticize Germany's decision to opt out of nuclear energy have fallen victim to the caterpillar's mistake: as it emerges from the chrysalis, it laments the disappearance of the cocoon because it has no premonition of the butterfly of renewable energy that it is destined to become.

16. It's Time to Get Angry, Europe. Create the Europe of Citizens Now!

Implementing democratic rights involves and requires many paths, arms, channels and guarantees – supranational, transnational, national and local. Can the democratic empowerment of a cosmopolitan Europe be accompanied by a strengthening of its national democracies in the member states?

17. Powerless but Legitimate: The Occupy Movement in the Financial Crisis

There is a surplus of power and a dearth of legitimacy on the side of capital and the states and a dearth of power and high legitimacy on the side of the Occupy movement. That is an imbalance which the movement could use to press home its core demands in the enlightened self-interest of the nation states and against their own narrow-mindedness.

18. Cooperate or Bust! The Existential Crisis of the European Union

European sociology needs to understand the modernization of other societies for supplementary reasons, in order to complete its worldview. It is rather the case that we Europeans can understand ourselves only if we 'deprovincialize' – in other words, if we learn to see through the eyes of others as a matter of sociological method.

19. What Is Meant by Global Domestic Politics?

Global domestic politics is not a normative concept but refers to a rampantly spreading, wild reality above, below and between the national borders which continue to dominate minds and institutions. Such a new global domestic political wilderness cannot be arrived at deductively (as an inference from a normative philosophy) but must instead be discovered and explored from below, from the mole perspective.

20. The Five Self-Delusions of a Supposedly Unpolitical Age

The national outlook not only misunderstands reality but it obscures how breathtakingly exciting sociology could become once again. The early sociologists were fascinated by the newly discovered, but yet to be surveyed, continent called society.

If one looks for conceptual commonalities among these snapshots from the everyday scenarios of global domestic politics, one can discover (at least) three characteristics. Global domestic politics denotes a new type of reflexive constellation:

(a) Here 'reflexive' must not be misunderstood in normative terms and confused with questions of philosophical ethics.
(b) Key institutions and actors in national and international politics are failing and this failure is becoming increasingly a matter of public aware-

ness and is being met with disenchantment with politics.

(c) The awareness of being increasingly closely interconnected by no means only fosters mutual understanding; it also globalizes fear and justifies, indeed stokes, bitter enmities and conflicts.

(a) Global domestic politics means a reflexive *conditio humana* in which the seemingly ontologically determined conception of 'separate worlds', the distinction between 'us' and 'the others', is no longer applicable. The opposition between a 'we' who live here and 'the others' who live there, the geographical, cultural, social and political separation between the 'native' and the 'foreign', is *de facto* falling to pieces. In the age of risk and the Internet, the world is becoming the everyday reference horizon, the space of new inequalities and new possibilities of action, independently of whether actors know it, want it, use it or merely suffer it and lament and combat it as a loss of autonomy and identity. All actors – migrants, companies, religious communities, human rights movements, researchers, workers, teachers, doctors, climatologists, members of 'global families', though also criminals and, not to forget, neonationalists and Al Qaeda terrorists – have to broaden their horizons of perception and action, make active comparisons, adopt the perspectives of others and coordinate them for their own purposes. That is what I mean by reflexive *conditio humana*. This new kind of historical compulsion to reflect, to shift perspectives across boundaries, often also with reference to the global public interest, however, must not be confused with *normativity*, with the big questions of philosophical ethics also raised by this concept, namely, 'What is "human"?' 'What is "humanity"?'

To take an example, the 'humanitarian interventions' which are supposed to help implement the human rights regime by military means constitute a genuine component of global domestic politics, even though the normative-philosophical and political-legal institutions at present exist only in fragments. There is no (really effective) global legal jurisdiction, no globally operating forces which could intervene in other states like a global police force, and no means of guaranteeing democratic state-formation.

Thus really existing global domestic politics does not have an answer to the daunting ethical question: are – or, more precisely, under which conditions are – humanitarian interventions justified, reprehensible or mandatory? But it does have an answer to the question of why the question of the justification of humanitarian interventions is on the agenda throughout the world and why instead of initiating a learning process it prompts manifold conflicts.

This distinction between a normative philosophical – 'pure' – global domestic politics, as understood, for example, by Carl Friedrich von Weizsäcker, and really existing – 'impure' – global domestic politics, which is experiencing an explosive development behind the façades of normality of national politics, is essential because the observation instruments of a global domestic politics understood in a universalistic philosophical sense have long since lost their analytical innocence in the turmoil of the conflict dynamics of global domestic politics.

(b) Global domestic politics represents a transitional stage between 'no longer' and 'not yet'. The old national-international institutions have ceased to function and new institutions – for example, the G-8 and the G-20 – have not yet been formally implemented and hence are still non-binding.

In the meantime it is a truism that, in view of the globalization of capital and risks, national measures are condemned to failure. A 'world state' does not exist and no international organization is in a position to regulate risks and flows of capital at the global level even approximately as efficiently as the welfare state during the nation state era of post-war continental Europe. Global domestic politics accordingly means the struggle over more complex instruments of political power beyond the nation state in the light of new forms of global political (inter)dependence. The terrain of world politics is developing in the field of tension between coordinated national policies, bilateral and multilateral treaties, international, transnational and supranational institutions, transnational corporations and private civil society foundations and networks. In spite of the rapid increase in number of global players, uneasiness is growing over the hesitant reactions to the global financial crisis, over the threatened sovereign default of certain EU countries, over the threat to the euro (and hence perhaps to the EU), but above all also over the disappointing results of the Copenhagen climate conference – an uneasiness, among other things, over the fact that these institutions are proving to be incapable of meeting the challenges for which they were created.

Can the World Bank overcome global poverty? Can the UN Food and Agriculture Organization (FAO) handle a global food crisis? Can the World Trade Organization (WTO) regulate global trade? Everything speaks for the fact that these institutions are far from being able to cope with the global risks and crises. Similar developments and disappointments can be observed at the national level with regard to democratic institutions and social security systems, though also when it comes to the institution of the family.

What does this mean for the conflict dynamics through which, in view of increasing national and global social inequalities, questions of social justice are being stirred up and are becoming ubiquitous in the struggle over the creation of transnational regimes and institutions? Where and how do practically effective forms of resistance, activity and alliance arise that go beyond mere lip service? More at the centre or the periphery?

More at the top or the bottom? More under coercion than voluntarily? Is the diversity of paths and constellations of dependence and interdependence of global domestic politics a suitable means to counteract the universalizing pressure exerted by a globalizing economy, by the global proliferation of human rights or even by the cosmopolitan imperative of world risk society? How can 'imagined cosmopolitan communities of risk' be created across territorial borders and social cleavages that open up new possibilities of communication and action?

(c) Global domestic politics is characterized by a *cosmopolitan dialectic*. Let me again use an example to explain this. The more climate change transforms the separate worlds in the world into fora of global domestic politics, the more extreme become the oppositions between North and South, rich and poor, developing and highly developed countries and regions. This has long since ceased to be just a matter of globalization. The issue is the power to canonize the correct path, the power to define what is right and wrong, good and evil, risky and safe in the globalized world. The concept 'really existing global domestic politics' is indispensable for describing these fierce conflicts, because the contradictory appeals to 'humanity' and the 'world' have become an everyday phenomenon in the social, political and moral domains. This is why the shift in perspective – the 'paradigm shift' – from a national worldview, which breaks down into domestic and foreign policy, to a worldview of global domestic politics driven by the hunger for reality is necessary at the observer level.

Moreover, the national outlook gives rise to fateful false alarms. How does climate change radicalize social inequalities within national contexts and at the global level? How does it separate winners from losers across the various internal and external borders? In order to be able even to approach these questions we must break open the misleading framework which focuses narrowly on 'gross national product' or 'per capita income' into which the problem of inequality is usually forced. Accordingly, attention must be focused on the fateful confluence of poverty, social vulnerability, corruption, the accumulation of dangers and the loss of dignity.

In the eyes of the poor inhabitants of the South, the turn from national to global domestic politics – the fact that 'the global other is in our midst' – expresses a twofold asymmetry. They are suffering the most but they are the ones who have contributed the least to global warming and who are least able to undertake anything against the catastrophic climate change. What significance did the Copenhagen climate summit in December 2000 have for them? Was it a disaster or a unique opportunity to be able to articulate and gain a global hearing for their role as victims in the first place?

To what extent do the 'cultural wounds' inflicted by colonialism play a role in the global domestic political conflicts? Was the Copenhagen summit a failure because countries such as Brazil, South Africa and India were welded together by their status as postcolonial nations? Like the Chinese, they argued that it was fundamentally unjust to prescribe lower levels of CO_2 emissions for the poorer countries than those of the United States and the EU, indeed all the more unjust because the industrialized West is responsible for the climate risks under which they are suffering.

A joke which made the rounds at the conference captures the point well: the United States and the EU are behaving like heedless rich people who have gorged themselves without restraint and now invite their neighbours to a cup of coffee and call on them to share the costs for the harm caused – appealing to the common good of the world.

It is paradoxical that the discussions over a global domestic politics are centred on and shaped by a Euro-American perspective. They investigate the multilayered phenomena of globalization, deal with shared risks, rights and responsibilities in a highly interdependent and simultaneously radically unequal world, but disproportionately they reflect the perspective of the old centre (and of Western-educated elites from the former colonies). In this way at least three deficiencies and errors creep into the discussion in principle.

First, the perspective of the poor countries is at a disadvantage so that, even when the focus is on plurality and diversity, the diagnoses of global domestic politics are largely rooted in the West.

Second, the observers' own cultural and political context of emergence is neglected and refuge is sought in universalism, so that the complications and confusions of a really existing global domestic politics remain unanalysed.

Third, because the assumptions originate in the orderly realities of the West, a worldview dominates which, contrary to all (inter)dependencies, conceives of the emerging social and political landscapes as more systematic than they really are.

The *Twenty Observations on a World in Turmoil* represents my far from adequate attempt to overcome these deficiencies.*

* All those readers who would like to form a more detailed picture of the empirical findings and the theoretical approaches and perspectives on the topic are recommended to read the special issue of the *British Journal of Sociology* (3/2010) entitled *Varieties of Second Modernity*.

20

The Five Self-Delusions of a Supposedly Unpolitical Age

Current political debates are dominated by positions which declare political action to be 'out of the question', 'pointless', 'impossible'. The more clearly the bewildering news reports document the emergence of a global domestic politics, the more blatantly the various intellectual cliques fall back upon the five self-delusions of the supposedly unpolitical age. These five positions differ above all with regard to how much politics they even allow.

1. The self-delusion of unpolitical globalization

A first self-delusion – it might be called the self-delusion of the globalized world – is expressed in the statement: 'No one can do politics against the markets.' Joschka Fischer's dictum was emblematic of the self-image of the political class over the past two decades. The politicians saw themselves as pawns in a power game dominated by globally operating capital. Here we are dealing with a self-delusion of unpolitical innocence in a twofold sense.

On the one hand, it glosses over the fact that the political class itself brought about the alleged powerlessness to act through its own conduct. Specifically, it imposed the rules of the globalized markets at the national level under the banner of 'reform policy', thus giving rise to the allegedly no longer controllable 'globalization destiny'. Note that global capital acquires its 'unchallengeable' power only when politics actively colludes in its own self-abolition.

On the other hand, the self-inflicted impotence of politics serves as a convenient excuse to deflect the pressure to act within global domestic politics and not to make use of the opportunities for action that are opening up. The argument runs as follows: since there are not, indeed there cannot be, any global political answers to the consequences of globalization, *there's nothing to be done*!

However, there is also the strategic option of standing the argument outlined on its head: then politicians raise expectations which everyone actually knows cannot be fulfilled. Before a G-20 summit, for example, loud calls are heard (with one eye on national audiences) for some kind of tax on global financial markets, in the certain knowledge that this has no chance of being implemented. Thus the motto: 'Everything must be regulated at the global level – and hence there's nothing to be done!' makes the deliberate uncoupling of talk from action possible. The more unattainable the proclaimed goal, the more blithely one can heap on demands and profile oneself as a champion of the global good, beautiful and necessary – without any fear of having to get one's hands dirty. Here the rhetoric of the new departure enters into an (un)canny marriage with the defence of the status quo.

Thus it makes complete sense when the German government joins the chorus of demands for a tax on financial transactions (a kind of value added tax on the financial industry) without for a moment believing that it will be introduced. Here the political strategy of the 'transposed heads' is at work, namely, that of overcoming the unpolitical age rhetorically only to confirm it in action. Distinguishing oneself and scoring points by presenting demands on the global stage in this way is possible as long as the assumption is shared that this cannot be achieved at the national level because those affected by corresponding measures in other countries could evade them and a global consensus about them does not exist. At the same time, viable alternatives are left out of consideration.

However, the alleged inability to act is contradicted by the globally coordinated 'grand politics' (Nietzsche) involved in rescuing 'system-relevant' banks and establishing assistance funds for countries threatened with bankruptcy. The 'hyper-activity' shown by states when confronted with the catastrophic self-destructive tendencies of capitalism makes a mockery of their unpolitical self-image. The permanent upward revision of ever more extravagant numbers, the disappearance into thin air of gigantic sums that originally were never there, lead to a devaluation of politics through hyperbole. Even if the 'rescue packages' were not the result of political coordination, but instead followed informal agreements and the egoistic agendas of individual states, these events nevertheless revealed for at least the blink of a global eye the political added value which, when mobilized by the need to avert perceived dangers to humanity, can propel political action like a rocket even in the otherwise so dogged, resistant and crisis-torn national arenas.

The problem is not the goal – the self-empowerment of politics through the experience of transnational cooperation – but the path leading to it, namely, overcoming the national ontology.

2. The national self-delusion

The national self-delusion rests on the assumption that there could be a return to the nation state idyll within existing global domestic politics. Thus everywhere we hear the lament that Europe is a faceless bureaucracy, Europe is decimating democracy, and Europe is undermining national diversity. There may be much that is right in this criticism, but it becomes false once it takes as its principle: no democracy without a nation. According to this nation state logic, a postnational Europe is necessarily a post-democratic Europe – which implies, conversely: the more EU, the less democracy.

This argument is false for a whole variety of reasons – and one can use it to show quite clearly how blinkered the national vision is. First, its proponents fail to appreciate that the route to a democratic Europe cannot be identical with the one pursued by the national democracies. Even the concept of democracy that serves as a standard for the EU must be a different one. The EU is made up of democratic states, but is not a state in the traditional sense. With this it becomes questionable, second, whether the models of democracy developed for the modern state can be extended to the EU or whether different, postnational approaches must be conceived in order to confer democratic legitimacy on European politics.

Both the absolutization of the concept of democracy tailored to the nation state and the failure to understand the unique historical path pursued by the democratization of Europe are rooted in the nostalgic self-delusion which absolutizes the national. Associated with this is the ardour with which the model of the 'social market economy' is extolled as the answer to the challenges of globalization, a policy approach which remains entirely in thrall to Keynesian national welfare policy. The current global domestic political constellation calls for a 'Keynes II' to revise 'Keynes I' in the light of global domestic politics. This new master thinker would have to develop a theory of the environmentally responsive, highly innovative, diversified economy which accords the global marketplace central importance within the horizon of global domestic politics.

3. The neoliberal self-delusion

Closely associated with the national self-delusion is the neoliberal self-delusion. In the post-Cold War era, neoliberal globalization has become the decisive normative and political force in global domestic politics. At the altars of the omnipotent market deity the promise is intoned time and again that all those who prostrate themselves before the imperatives of the global market will be blessed with earthly riches. Ultimately, neoliberalism claims to be the better socialism because it is supposed to be possible with the aid of the global market regime (and only with its aid) to overcome poverty and create a more just world not only at the national but also at the global level. Thus, neoliberalism has established itself as a kind of global political party which exercises influence within the different national parties and political arenas, but in doing so claims to represent not the interests of business but global values.

As emphatically recorded in the observations collected in this volume, global risks (climate change, financial crises, terrorism, though also the cloud of volcanic ash and the oil disaster in the Gulf of Mexico) are plunging the system created by the neoliberal coalition of capital and the state into disarray. Global risks empower states and new social movements because they bring new sources of legitimation and practical options to light; on the other hand, they are disempowering globalized capital because the consequences of investment decisions are now giving rise to incalculable and life-threatening global risks.

Among the most revealing indicators of how and how much the neoliberal utopia of global transformation has turned out to be a self-delusion is the 'conversion effect'.

Even those political parties and heads of government who propagated the norms of 'good housekeeping' (low inflation, a balanced budget, dismantling trade barriers and foreign exchange controls, maximum freedom of movement of capital, minimal regulation of the labour market and a lean, flexible state which impels its citizens to work) as a 'reform programme' prior to the financial crisis are now proclaiming, both at home and abroad, that for which Oskar Lafontaine, the former SPD finance minister in the Schröder government, was castigated, namely, the need to impose a regulatory straitjacket on globally operating financial capital.

4. The neo-Marxist self-delusion

Capitalism has gone haywire and is threatening to plunge whole countries into chaos. No wonder that many, and even some outstanding voices feel vindicated in their judgement that, although Marx got some of the details wrong, he was right for the most part. These neocommunist intellectuals, who likewise have a leaning towards nationalism, are lending their support to a thoroughly crisis-ridden, but nevertheless thoroughly unrevolutionary and unreformable global capitalism. In this view, all parties are congregating around the so-called 'Golden Mean', a kind of place of longing far removed from all extremes in which only a perfectly pragmatic and efficient reason is supposed to rule. In this way, as the light-hearted, postmodern communists see it, the subsumption of politics under capital is once again being perfected.

Ironically enough, the neo-Marxist self-delusion is the ugly twin sister of the neoliberal self-delusion. The harshest critics of global capitalism, of all people, are becoming apologists for the neoliberal global market state. For them, too, the (welfare) state is undergoing a self-transformation, but exclusively in the sense of the self-accommodation of national politics to the dominance of the global market, which ultimately amounts to the self-liquidation of politics. However, neo-Marxists and neoliberals attach diametrically opposed values to the resulting global situation.

It follows that, from the perspective of the neo-Marxists, the globalization of capital is by no means giving rise to an ambivalent global domestic politics, neither *de facto* nor in the normative, philosophical sense. On the contrary, it remains the case that economics prescribes the sound barrier which cannot be broken through by politics because it is and remains the handmaid of economics. This fails to appreciate the political character of global domestic politics. The global economy breaks open the national economic power container, forces countries to open their borders and conquers the resulting space of power of global domestic politics. However, the neo-Marxist field of vision is blind to the fact that the shock of global domestic politics also gives rise to new fields, resources and possibilities of action for all actors both inside and outside national borders. On the contrary, the state is becoming the colony of global economic domination.

In this way, global domestic political tensions and fissures which have been triggered within global capitalism by the financial crisis go unrecognized. I have in mind especially the emergence of a new capitalism with Asian-Pacific, Latin American variants and hues. This has progressively developed into the alternative system to the shattered arrogance of the West, which equates the global victory of capitalism with the global victory of neoliberalism.

Why does this represent a self-delusion (of the neo-Marxists and of the West in general)? Because it blinds its adherents to how the financial crisis and climate change have demystified and delegitimized the Western creed of modernity. The neo-Marxist self-delusion distorts one's view of the central fact of global domestic politics: the modernist creed has become contingent with regard to ideology, politics, institutions and expectations concerning continuity, though also not least with regard to the daunting questions of 'what is "human"?' and 'what is "humanity"?'.

The Western elites embrace the article of faith that the financial crisis is a system failure (thus they concede that there has been failure), but nobody is to blame for it. Will permissive capitalism have to change in the future? The history of crises teaches us: not really! The institutions and paradigms are resistant to change, the pendulum of the market forces is swinging back, mass consumption behaviour has not really changed and the pressure for reform is already water under the bridge.

The situation in global domestic politics presents a completely different picture in the eyes of the developing countries. It is marked by:

– a shift in power in favour of the developing countries (which is also reflected, among other things, in their participation in the new G-20 summit);

– a displacement of the centre of gravity of the geography of power within the global economy from the Atlantic to the Pacific region;

– the creeping de-monopolization of the US dollar as the global reserve currency in favour of a bundle of different currencies and bilateral monetary agreements;

– the growing importance of South–South and East–South cooperation when it comes to solving economic problems; and, last but not least,

– the loss in moral authority and exemplariness of the old Euro-American centre.

The backward-looking notions of continuity of the neo-Marxists (and the neoliberals) according to which the developing countries remain prisoners of the radical capitalist creed is hindering the insight into the new competition among systems. This no longer pits capitalism against socialism but different alternatives within capitalism against each other. This raises the key question: which development scenarios and perspectives does divided, multiple, multipolar, more or less regulated capitalism offer in view of global risks? A nonnostalgic Left which extends and renews the concept of politics in a transnational direction is nowhere in sight.

5. The technocratic self-delusion

If the positions discussed so far presuppose a minimization of the political options, the technocratic position seeks to maximize the political scope for action in the face of the threats to humanity. Climatologists are without doubt impeccable realists but in social and political matters they are often idealists because they regard all human beings as lay climatologists, and thus cannot understand why their apocalyptic model calculations do not automatically trigger the urgently required countermeasures.

This is how the technocratic self-delusion arises. For in the world of *Homo oecologicus*, the primacy of democracy becomes secondary and the disparities caused by climate change and climate policy become inconsequential. This leads to the danger of jumping directly from the chillingly beautiful images of melting ice caps to the need for a kind of crisis expertocracy which accords the well-being of the planet priority over national egoisms and democratic reservations in the interest of survival.

The three components – the anticipation of the calamity engulfing humanity, the time constraints, and the manifest inability of democracies to undertake decisive measures – ensure that the most committed individuals in particular are fixated half-unspokenly on Wolfgang Harich's vision of the 'strong, resolute allocation and ascetic distribution state', and hence on models of environmental dictatorship. This raises the key question: how is democracy possible in a time of climate change? Or to put it even more bluntly: why is the advancement of democracy a *conditio sine qua non* for a cosmopolitan politics of climate change?

The technocratic self-delusion is predicated on single states actively imposing an environmental dictatorship. But how do states force other states to embrace the eco-consensus? Through wars? Through a global environmental dictatorship? Here at the latest it becomes evident that the technocratic self-delusion not only negates the values of democracy and freedom but is in the end ineffectual, even counter-productive.

6. Conclusion: the politics of the unpolitical is no longer viable

The confusion of existing global domestic politics is disrupting and destroying the self-image of the unpolitical age. Two diametrically opposed futures are looming. One is a Hegel scenario in which the threats engendered by global risk capitalism represent a historical opportunity for the 'cunning of reason'. This is the cosmopolitan imperative: cooperate or fail, succeed together or fail alone.

At the same time, however, the everyday experience that the world is becoming uncontrollable also triggers a Carl Schmitt scenario, a strategic power game which, as the planetary state of exception is becoming normalized, dismantles basic rights and democracy and opens the doors for a neonationalist politics. Remarkably, these mutually contradictory potential futures seem to be interconnected in a variety of ways; this used to be called 'dialectics'.

On the one hand, new fora – G-8, G-20 – are emerging in which the simultaneously local, national and global problems should be defined in such a way that they are capable of being negotiated and acted upon. On the other hand, the G-8 of the industrial countries including Russia could barely reach an agreement on the financial system, climate change or social standards, for example. Now China, India and other emerging countries are making their voices heard and cross-cutting lines of conflict are emerging at the roundtable of the G-20 summit: rich countries against poorer countries, stable countries against debtor countries, Anglo-Saxon capitalism against the social market economy on the Rhine and the Seine. And looming over it all is the new competition between the democracies and the authoritarian capitalist regimes flush with success extending from China through the Arab countries to South America.

It's no wonder that the business in hopelessness is flourishing. But how do prospects assume concrete form? Given this turmoil and stalemate, can the cosmopolitical imperative ('cooperate or bust!') develop into a power resource to break through the dominant fatalism of the unpolitical and to make it possible to mobilize a majority for the primacy of the political at the transnational level?

Yet all of this ultimately raises questions concerning a new normative-political global domestic politics: who is actually authorized to make justified decisions and to create institutions capable of bringing international financial flows under control? What kind of consensus is needed and who must be involved in order to confront the worldwide catastrophe of climate change? Can the fight (or failure to fight) against AIDS, in which the lives of millions are at stake, be decided in the private sphere under conditions of unaccountability? Which type of political actor or political institution should ideally be conceived for this purpose and at which level and equipped with which kind of mandate?

How are global, transnational, national and local decision-making powers related, while nevertheless remaining distinct from each other? Who lays down which transnational norms and regulations should be followed above the heads of (but nevertheless binding on) nation states, and who is authorized to do so on what basis?

One thing is clear: the national outlook not only misunderstands this reality but it obscures how breathtakingly exciting sociology could become once again. The early sociologists were fascinated by the newly discovered, but yet to be surveyed, continent called society. A reflection of this fascination could reappear if the curiosity of discovering and testing the unexplored landscapes, enthusiasms, contradictions and dilemmas of existing global domestic politics and its resources and perspectives for governance and action were to revive the sociological imagination and made sociology interesting once again.

K 95 M   KITCH

8 95

203704